THE NATURE OF SCIENCE

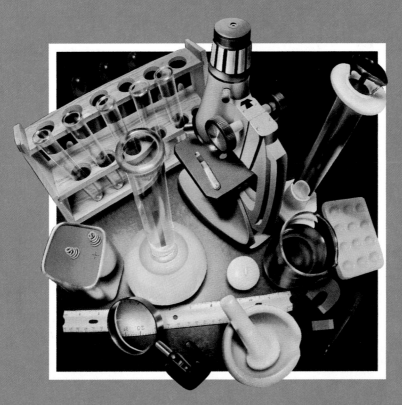

Anthea Maton
Former NSTA National Coordinator
Project Scope, Sequence, Coordination
Washington, DC

Jean Hopkins
Science Instructor and Department Chairperson
John H. Wood Middle School
San Antonio, Texas

Susan Johnson
Professor of Biology
Ball State University
Muncie, Indiana

David LaHart
Senior Instructor
Florida Solar Energy Center
Cape Canaveral, Florida

Charles William McLaughlin
Science Instructor and Department Chairperson
Central High School
St. Joseph, Missouri

Maryanna Quon Warner
Science Instructor
Del Dios Middle School
Escondido, California

Jill D. Wright
Professor of Science Education
Director of International Field Programs
University of Pittsburgh
Pittsburgh, Pennsylvania

Prentice Hall
Englewood Cliffs, New Jersey
Needham, Massachusetts

Prentice Hall Science

The Nature of Science

Student Text and Annotated Teacher's Edition
Laboratory Manual
Teacher's Resource Package
Teacher's Desk Reference
Computer Test Bank
Teaching Transparencies
Product Testing Activities
Computer Courseware
Video and Interactive Video

The illustration on the cover, rendered by Keith Kasnot, depicts some of the variety of tools used in the exploration of the natural world.

Credits begin on page 124.

SECOND EDITION

ISBN 0-13-400409-4

2 3 4 5 6 7 8 9 10   97 96 95 94 93

Prentice Hall
A Division of Simon & Schuster
Englewood Cliffs, New Jersey 07632

STAFF CREDITS

Editorial:	Harry Bakalian, Pamela E. Hirschfeld, Maureen Grassi, Robert P. Letendre, Elisa Mui Eiger, Lorraine Smith-Phelan, Christine A. Caputo
Design:	AnnMarie Roselli, Carmela Pereira, Susan Walrath, Leslie Osher, Art Soares
Production:	Suse F. Bell, Joan McCulley, Elizabeth Torjussen, Christina Burghard
Photo Research:	Libby Forsyth, Emily Rose, Martha Conway
Publishing Technology:	Andrew Grey Bommarito, Deborah Jones, Monduane Harris, Michael Colucci, Gregory Myers, Cleasta Wilburn
Marketing:	Andrew Socha, Victoria Willows
Pre-Press Production:	Laura Sanderson, Kathryn Dix, Denise Herckenrath
Manufacturing:	Rhett Conklin, Gertrude Szyferblatt

Consultants

Kathy French	National Science Consultant
Jeannie Dennard	National Science Consultant
Brenda Underwood	National Science Consultant
Janelle Conarton	National Science Consultant

Contributing Writers

Linda Densman
Science Instructor
Hurst, TX

Linda Grant
Former Science Instructor
Weatherford, TX

Heather Hirschfeld
Science Writer
Durham, NC

Marcia Mungenast
Science Writer
Upper Montclair, NJ

Michael Ross
Science Writer
New York City, NY

Content Reviewers

Dan Anthony
Science Mentor
Rialto, CA

John Barrow
Science Instructor
Pomona, CA

Leslie Bettencourt
Science Instructor
Harrisville, RI

Carol Bishop
Science Instructor
Palm Desert, CA

Dan Bohan
Science Instructor
Palm Desert, CA

Steve M. Carlson
Science Instructor
Milwaukie, OR

Larry Flammer
Science Instructor
San Jose, CA

Steve Ferguson
Science Instructor
Lee's Summit, MO

Robin Lee Harris Freedman
Science Instructor
Fort Bragg, CA

Edith H. Gladden
Former Science Instructor
Philadelphia, PA

Vernita Marie Graves
Science Instructor
Tenafly, NJ

Jack Grube
Science Instructor
San Jose, CA

Emiel Hamberlin
Science Instructor
Chicago, IL

Dwight Kertzman
Science Instructor
Tulsa, OK

Judy Kirschbaum
Science/Computer Instructor
Tenafly, NJ

Kenneth L. Krause
Science Instructor
Milwaukie, OR

Ernest W. Kuehl, Jr.
Science Instructor
Bayside, NY

Mary Grace Lopez
Science Instructor
Corpus Christi, TX

Warren Maggard
Science Instructor
PeWee Valley, KY

Della M. McCaughan
Science Instructor
Biloxi, MS

Stanley J. Mulak
Former Science Instructor
Jensen Beach, FL

Richard Myers
Science Instructor
Portland, OR

Carol Nathanson
Science Mentor
Riverside, CA

Sylvia Neivert
Former Science Instructor
San Diego, CA

Jarvis VNC Pahl
Science Instructor
Rialto, CA

Arlene Sackman
Science Instructor
Tulare, CA

Christine Schumacher
Science Instructor
Pikesville, MD

Suzanne Steinke
Science Instructor
Towson, MD

Len Svinth
Science Instructor/ Chairperson
Petaluma, CA

Elaine M. Tadros
Science Instructor
Palm Desert, CA

Joyce K. Walsh
Science Instructor
Midlothian, VA

Steve Weinberg
Science Instructor
West Hartford, CT

Charlene West, PhD
Director of Curriculum
Rialto, CA

John Westwater
Science Instructor
Medford, MA

Glenna Wilkoff
Science Instructor
Chesterfield, OH

Edee Norman Wiziecki
Science Instructor
Urbana, IL

Teacher Advisory Panel

Beverly Brown
Science Instructor
Livonia, MI

James Burg
Science Instructor
Cincinnati, OH

Karen M. Cannon
Science Instructor
San Diego, CA

John Eby
Science Instructor
Richmond, CA

Elsie M. Jones
Science Instructor
Marietta, GA

Michael Pierre McKereghan
Science Instructor
Denver, CO

Donald C. Pace, Sr.
Science Instructor
Reisterstown, MD

Carlos Francisco Sainz
Science Instructor
National City, CA

William Reed
Science Instructor
Indianapolis, IN

Multicultural Consultant

Steven J. Rakow
Associate Professor
University of Houston— Clear Lake
Houston, TX

English as a Second Language (ESL) Consultants

Jaime Morales
Bilingual Coordinator
Huntington Park, CA

Pat Hollis Smith
Former ESL Instructor
Beaumont, TX

Reading Consultant

Larry Swinburne
Director
Swinburne Readability Laboratory

CONTENTS

THE NATURE OF SCIENCE

Activity Bank/Reference Section

Features

CONCEPT MAPPING

Throughout your study of science, you will learn a variety of terms, facts, figures, and concepts. Each new topic you encounter will provide its own collection of words and ideas—which, at times, you may think seem endless. But each of the ideas within a particular topic is related in some way to the others. No concept in science is isolated. Thus it will help you to understand the topic if you see the whole picture; that is, the interconnectedness of all the individual terms and ideas. This is a much more effective and satisfying way of learning than memorizing separate facts.

Actually, this should be a rather familiar process for you. Although you may not think about it in this way, you analyze many of the elements in your daily life by looking for relationships or connections. For example, when you look at a collection of flowers, you may divide them into groups: roses, carnations, and daisies. You may then associate colors with these flowers: red, pink, and white. The general topic is flowers. The subtopic is types of flowers. And the colors are specific terms that describe flowers. A topic makes more sense and is more easily understood if you understand how it is broken down into individual ideas and how these ideas are related to one another and to the entire topic.

It is often helpful to organize information visually so that you can see how it all fits together. One technique for describing related ideas is called a **concept map**. In a concept map, an idea is represented by a word or phrase enclosed in a box. There are several ideas in any concept map. A connection between two ideas is made with a line. A word or two that describes the connection is written on or near the line. The general topic is located at the top of the map. That topic is then broken down into subtopics, or more specific ideas, by branching lines. The most specific topics are located at the bottom of the map.

To construct a concept map, first identify the important ideas or key terms in the chapter or section. Do not try to include too much information. Use your judgment as to what is really important. Write the general topic at the top of your map. Let's use an example to help illustrate this process. Suppose you decide that the key terms in a section you are reading are School, Living Things, Language Arts, Subtraction, Grammar, Mathematics, Experiments, Papers, Science, Addition, Novels. The general topic is School. Write and enclose this word in a box at the top of your map.

SCHOOL

Now choose the subtopics—Language Arts, Science, Mathematics. Figure out how they are related to the topic. Add these words to your map. Continue this procedure until you have included all the important ideas and terms. Then use lines to make the appropriate connections between ideas and terms. Don't forget to write a word or two on or near the connecting line to describe the nature of the connection.

Do not be concerned if you have to redraw your map (perhaps several times!) before you show all the important connections clearly. If, for example, you write papers for Science as well as for Language Arts, you may want to place these two subjects next to each other so that the lines do not overlap.

One more thing you should know about concept mapping: Concepts can be correctly mapped in many different ways. In fact, it is unlikely that any two people will draw identical concept maps for a complex topic. Thus there is no one correct concept map for any topic! Even

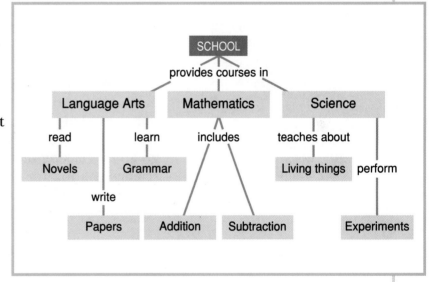

though your concept map may not match those of your classmates, it will be correct as long as it shows the most important concepts and the clear relationships among them. Your concept map will also be correct if it has meaning to you and if it helps you understand the material you are reading. A concept map should be so clear that if some of the terms are erased, the missing terms could easily be filled in by following the logic of the concept map.

THE NATURE OF SCIENCE

▲ Science has provided us with computer chips and circuits, which are used in modern electronic equipment.

Do you read the newspaper or watch the news on television? Perhaps you prefer the radio or even science magazines. Whatever your preference, you know that it's hard to escape hearing about advances in science.

Computers, CD players, microwave ovens, and even hand-held video games all became possible through discoveries in science. Science, for better or for worse, is all around us. It is through science that we have developed new sources of energy—and have found ways to make traditional sources more efficient and less polluting. Science has given us television, telephones, and other forms of communication. A list of scientific advances that have improved our lives could fill this textbook alone!

What exactly is science? How do scientists go about making discoveries? If you think that science is a job for white-coated laboratory workers who never look up from their microscope or get involved in the world around

Not all the effects of science are positive. Here you see two well-protected scientists carrying hazardous wastes from a chemical spill. ▶

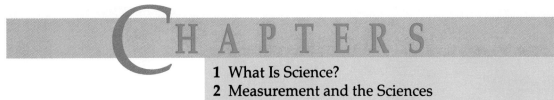

CHAPTERS

1 What Is Science?
2 Measurement and the Sciences
3 Tools and the Sciences

them, you're in for a surprise. In this textbook you will find out about the nature of science and the ways in which scientists investigate the world. You will have an opportunity to explore and discover a few things yourself. We hope you discover something that few people really understand: Science is fun. Now go to it—and enjoy!

▶ *It has been through the work of environmental scientists that people have begun to take seriously the threat to many of Earth's greatest creatures, among them the African elephant.*

Discovery *Activity*

What Is It?

1. Examine carefully a leaf (or another part of a plant), a magnifying glass, and a rock.

2. Write down a list of characteristics you would use to describe each of these objects. Your list should include size, color, texture, shape, and any other feature you feel is important.

3. Provide your description of each object to a parent or guardian without showing the actual object. See if the parent or guardian can determine what the object is by your description alone.

   ■ How helpful was your description? What sort of tools or instruments would have allowed you to describe each object better?

What Is Science?

Scientists, like most people, love a mystery. Recently, Dr. W. P. Coombs Jr., of Western New England College, was called upon to solve a most interesting puzzle. Strange scratches had been found on some rocks unearthed at the Connecticut State Dinosaur Park. Dr. Coombs is a dinosaur expert. He took one look at the scratches on the exposed rocks and immediately knew what they were—dinosaur footprints. The scratches appeared in groups of three, leading Dr. Coombs to conclude that the scratches were made by an animal having three toes with sharp claws. They were clearly the work of the meat-eating dinosaur called *Megalosaurus*.

There was something peculiar about the footprints. Only the tips of the dinosaur's toes seemed to have touched the rocks. But *Megalosaurus* did not run on its toes, at least not on land. Dr. Coombs quickly realized that the prints had been made under water, where most of the animal's weight would have been kept off the rocks. From scratches on rocks, Dr. Coombs had discovered the first evidence of a swimming, meat-eating dinosaur. Unearthed rocks, a sharp eye, and some smart detective work had led to an important scientific discovery.

Journal *Activity*

You and Your World Is this your first science course? Or are you an old hand at science? In either case, in your journal jot down your feelings about taking a science course. It might be interesting to go back to your entry at the end of the year and see if you still feel the same.

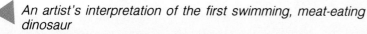

An artist's interpretation of the first swimming, meat-eating dinosaur

1–1 Science—Not Just for Scientists

You are a scientist! Does that statement surprise you? If it does, it is probably because you do not understand exactly what a scientist is. But if you have ever observed the colors formed in a drop of oil in a puddle or watched a fire burn, you were acting like a scientist. You are also a scientist when you watch waves breaking on the shore or lightning bolts darting through the night sky. Or perhaps you have walked through the grass in the morning and noticed drops of dew or have screamed with delight as you watched a roller coaster dipping up and down the track. Whenever you observe the world around you, you are acting like a scientist. Does that give you a clue to the nature of science and scientists?

Scientists observe the world around them—just as you do. For that reason, whenever you make an observation you are acting like a scientist. But scientists do more than just observe. The word *science* comes from the Latin *scire,* which means "to know." So science is more than just observation. And real scientists do more than just observe. They question what they see. They wonder what makes things the way they are. And they attempt to find answers to their questions.

No doubt you also wonder about and question what you see—at least some of the time. Hopefully, you will be better able to find answers to some of your questions as a result of reading this chapter. That is, you will be better able to approach the world as a scientist does.

Figure 1–1 *Whenever you observe and question natural occurrences, such as a lightning storm, you are acting as a scientist does.*

Figure 1–2 *The goal of science is to understand events that occur in the world around us—such as this rare desert snowstorm in Arizona.*

The Nature of Science

The universe around you and inside of you is really a collection of countless mysteries. It is the job of scientists to solve those mysteries. **The goal of science is to understand the world around us.**

How do scientists go about understanding the world? Like all good detectives, scientists use special methods to determine truths about nature. Such truths are called facts. Here is an example of a fact: The sun is a source of light and heat. But science is more than a list of facts—just as studying science is more than memorizing facts. Jules Henri Poincaré, a famous nineteenth-century French scientist who charted the motions of planets, put it this way: "Science is built up with facts, as a house is with stones. But a collection of facts is no more a science than a heap of stones is a house."

So scientists go further than simply discovering facts. Scientists try to use facts to solve larger mysteries of nature. In this sense, you might think of facts as clues to scientific mysteries. An example of a larger mystery is how the sun produces the heat and light it showers upon the Earth. Another larger mystery is how the relatively few and simple organisms of 3 billion years ago gave rise to the many complex organisms that inhabit the Earth today.

Using facts they have gathered, scientists propose explanations for the events they observe. Then they perform experiments to test their explanations. In the next section of this chapter, you will learn how scientists go about performing experiments and uncovering the mysteries of nature.

Reading a Food Label

You may wonder why studying science is important in your life. If you have ever read the ingredients on a food label, then you already know one reason. A knowledge of chemistry helps you learn what ingredients are in the foods you eat!

Look at the label on a box of cereal. The ingredients are listed, in order, by the amount present in the food.

Make a list of the ingredients that are present in the food label you are examining. Next to each ingredient indicate with a checkmark whether it is familiar to you.

■ Find out what each ingredient is and how the body uses it.

■ Which ingredients are preservatives?

Report your findings to your class.

Activity Bank

Observing a Fish, p.100

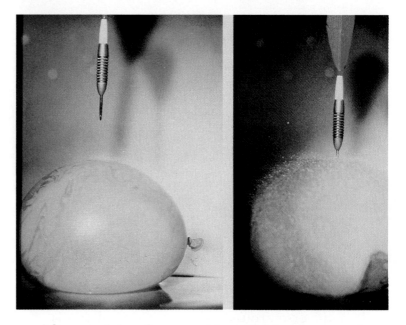

Figure 1–3 *It had long been a theory that a liquid did not retain its shape when removed from its container. However, scientists were forced to change that theory after observing the photographs shown here. The photographs show that the water in the balloon retained its balloon shape for 12 to 13 millionths of a second after the balloon had been burst by a dart.*

After studying facts, making observations, and performing experiments, scientists may develop a **theory.** A theory is the most logical explanation for events that occur in nature. Keep in mind that scientists do not use the word theory as you do. For example, you may have a theory about why your favorite soccer team is not winning. Your theory may or may not make sense. But it is not a scientific theory. A scientific theory is not just a guess or a hunch. A scientific theory is a powerful, time-tested concept that makes useful and dependable predictions about the natural world.

When a scientist proposes a theory, that theory must be tested over and over again. If it survives the

Figure 1–4 *Life science includes the study of animals such as the diamondback rattlesnake.*

tests, the theory may be accepted by the scientific community. However, theories can be wrong and may be changed after additional tests and/or observations.

If a theory survives many tests and is generally accepted as true, scientists may call it a **law.** However, as with theories, even scientific laws may change as new information is provided or new experiments are performed. This points out the spirit at the heart of science: Always allow questions to be asked and new scientific explanations to be considered.

Branches of Science

One of the skills you will develop as you continue to study science is the ability to organize things in a logical, orderly way—that is, to classify things. Classification systems are an important part of science. For example, biologists classify all life on Earth into five broad kingdoms of living things. Astronomers classify stars into five main types according to their size. And chemists classify the 109 known elements according to their properties, or characteristics.

Even the study of science can be classified into groups or, in this case, what we call branches of science. There can be many branches of science, each determined by the subject matter being studied. For our purposes, however, we will consider only the three main (overarching) branches of science: life science, earth science, and physical science.

LIFE SCIENCE   Life science deals with living things and their parts and actions. Smaller branches of life science include zoology (the study of animals) and botany (the study of plants).

EARTH SCIENCE   Earth science is the study of the Earth and its rocks, oceans, volcanoes, earthquakes, atmosphere, and other features. Usually earth science also includes astronomy. Astronomers explore nature beyond the Earth. They study such objects as stars, planets, and moons.

PHYSICAL SCIENCE   Physical science is the study of matter and energy. Some physical scientists explore what substances are made of and how they change

Figure 1–5 *What branch of science includes the study of planet Saturn?*

Figure 1–6 *Physics is the branch of physical science that studies the heat and light given off by a campfire. What branch of physical science would study the chemical changes that occur when wood burns?*

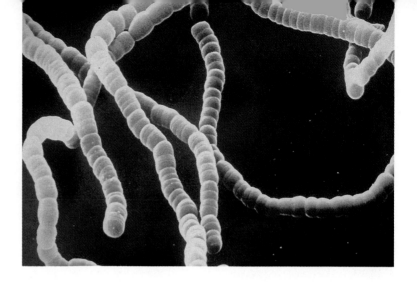

Figure 1–7 *Bacteria are among the living things examined by scientists who explore the microscopic world.*

and combine. This branch of physical science is called chemistry. Other physical scientists study forms of energy such as heat and light. This is the science of physics.

It is important for you to remember that the branches of science are a handy way to classify the subject matter scientists study. But it would be a mistake to think that any branch works independently of the others. To the contrary, the branches of science actually interweave and overlap most of the time. Science does not happen in a vacuum, and the great discoveries of science do not usually occur unless scientists from many branches work together.

Questions Scientists Ask

Even within a particular branch of science, the subjects studied are often quite specialized. Such specialization is usually based on the types of questions scientists might ask about their world. Let's see how this works.

QUESTIONS AT THE MICROSCOPIC LEVEL Many scientists seek truths about the microscopic world around them. Life scientists, for example, might ask how tiny bacteria invade the body and cause disease. Or they may try to determine how each cell in your body performs all of the functions necessary for life. Physical scientists may question how parts of an atom interact or why some chemical compounds are harmless while others are poisonous (toxic). Earth scientists examine the internal structure of rocks to determine why some rocks last for millions of years while others are worn away by wind and water in a matter of decades.

ACTIVITY
DISCOVERING

Homestyle Classification

Is classification only for scientists? Not at all. Choose a room in your home and take a careful look around. Make a list of the various ways in which objects are classified. (For example, all of your socks are probably grouped together in one drawer.)

■ Does this activity suggest ways in which you might classify objects in order to organize them better?

Figure 1-8 *Scientists who study volcanoes want to know not only why a volcano erupts but also how such eruptions can be predicted. Why is the ability to predict an eruption of great importance?*

QUESTIONS AT THE MACROSCOPIC LEVEL Other scientists search for answers to questions that involve the macroscopic world, or the world of objects visible to the unaided eye. Macroscopic questions usually involve large groups of objects. Earth scientists, for example, may want to determine the forces that caused a particular volcano to erupt or the causes of an earthquake in a certain area. Physical scientists may question why it takes longer to stop a heavy car than a light one. And life scientists might examine the populations of organisms in an area to determine how each organism interacts with other organisms and with the surrounding environment.

Figure 1-9 *Much of science deals with global issues. One such issue is the worldwide effects of pollution on our environment.*

QUESTIONS AT THE GLOBAL LEVEL Some of the questions scientists seek to answer have a more global or world viewpoint. Earth scientists, for example, may study wind patterns throughout the atmosphere in order to determine how weather can be more accurately predicted. Life scientists may seek to determine how pollutants poured into the air or water in one part of the world affect living things far off in another part of the world. And physical scientists may search for the fundamental forces in nature that govern all events in the universe.

As you can see, there are many types of questions to be answered and many areas of science you may wish to pursue in future years. But whether or not you want to become a scientist, you can still ask questions about your world and seek answers to those questions. The study of science is not restricted to scientists! Anyone with the curiosity to ask questions and the energy to seek answers can call a small part of science his or her own. Any takers?

1. What is the goal of science?
2. Describe the three main branches of science. Give an example of a question that might be asked by scientists in each branch.

Critical Thinking—*Applying Concepts*
3. How might advances in technology affect the kinds of questions scientists ask about the world?

Guide for Reading

Focus on these questions as you read.

▶ *What is the scientific method?*

▶ *How does it help scientists to discover truths about nature?*

1–2 The Scientific Method— A Way of Problem Solving

You have read about the goal of science, the branches of science, and the types of questions scientists ask. By now you may be wondering just what separates science from other subject areas. After all, historians ask questions about the causes of conflicts between nations, philosophers ask questions about the nature of existence, and experts on literature seek the hidden meaning and symbolism in great novels. In fact, just about every area of study asks questions about the world. So what's so special about science?

What distinguishes science from other fields of study is the way in which science seeks answers to questions. In other words, what separates science is an approach called the **scientific method.** The scientific method is a systematic approach to problem solving. **The basic steps in the scientific method are**

Stating the problem
Gathering information on the problem
Forming a hypothesis
Performing experiments to test the hypothesis
Recording and analyzing data
Stating a conclusion
Repeating the work

The following example shows how the scientific method was used to solve a problem. As you will see, the steps of the scientific method often overlap.

Stating the Problem

Bundled up in warm clothing, heads bent into the wind, two friends walked along the beach. Drifts of snow rose against the slats of a fence that in the summer held back dunes of sand. Beyond the fence, a row of beach houses drew the attention of the friends.

There, from the roofs of the houses, hung glistening strips of ice. Only yesterday these beautiful icicles had been a mass of melting snow. Throughout the night, the melted snow had continued to drip, freezing into lovely shapes.

Near the ocean's edge, the friends spied a small pool of sea water. Surprisingly, it was not frozen as were the icicles on the roofs. What could be the reason for this curious observation, the friends wondered?

Without realizing it, the friends had taken an important step in the scientific method. They had recognized a scientific problem. A scientist might state this problem in another way: What causes fresh water to freeze at a higher temperature than sea water?

ACTIVITY

WRITING

Changing Theories

Albert Einstein once stated that he would consider his work a failure if new and better theories did not replace his own. Using the following words, write an essay describing how new evidence can change an existing theory.

data
variable
hypothesis
scientific method
control
experiment
conclusions

Figure 1–10 *What causes fresh water to freeze at a higher temperature than sea water? How might you find an answer to this question?*

Gathering Information on the Problem

A scientist might begin to solve the problem by gathering information. The scientist would first find out how the sea water in the pool differs from the fresh water on the roof. This information might include the following facts: The pool of sea water rests on sand, while the fresh water drips along a tar roof. The sea water is exposed to the cold air for less time than the fresh water. The sea water is saltier than the fresh water.

Forming a Hypothesis

Using all of the information that has been gathered, the scientist might be prepared to suggest a possible solution to the problem. A proposed solution to a scientific problem is called a **hypothesis** (high-PAHTH-uh-sihs). A hypothesis almost always follows the gathering of information about a problem. But sometimes a hypothesis is a sudden idea that springs from a new and original way of looking at a problem.

Among the hypotheses that might be suggested as solutions to our problem is this: Because fresh water does not contain salt, it freezes at a higher temperature than sea water.

Performing Experiments to Test the Hypothesis

A scientist does not stop once a hypothesis has been suggested. In science, evidence that either supports a hypothesis or does not support it must be found. This means that a hypothesis must be tested to show whether or not it is correct. Such testing is usually done by performing experiments.

Experiments are performed according to specific rules. By following these rules, scientists can be confident that the evidence they uncover will clearly support or not support a hypothesis. For the problem of the sea water and fresh water, a scientist would have to design an experiment that ruled out every factor but salt as the cause of the different freezing temperatures.

Let's see how a scientist would actually do this. First, the scientist would put equal amounts of fresh water into two identical containers. Then the scientist would add salt to only one of the containers. The salt is the **variable,** or the factor being tested. In any experiment, only one variable should be tested at a time. In this way, the scientist can be fairly certain that the results of the experiment are caused by one and only one factor—in this case the variable of salt. To eliminate the possibility of hidden or unknown variables, the scientist must run a **control** experiment. A control experiment is set up exactly like the one that contains the variable. The only difference is that the control experiment does not contain the variable.

In this experiment, the scientist uses two containers of the same size with equal amounts of water. The water in both containers is at the same starting temperature. The containers are placed side by side in the freezing compartment of a refrigerator and checked every five minutes. *But only one container has salt in it.* In this way, the scientist can be fairly sure that any differences that occur in the two containers are due to the single variable of salt. In such experiments, the part of the experiment with the variable is called the experimental setup. The part of the experiment with the control is called the control setup.

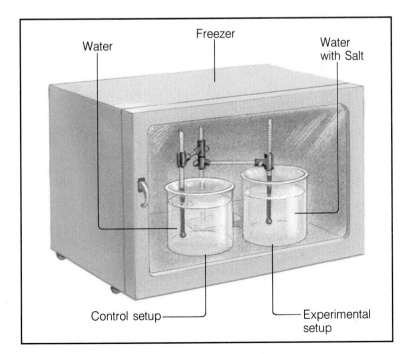

Figure 1–11 *What is the variable in this experiment? Explain your answer.*

Recording and Analyzing Data

To determine whether salt affects the freezing temperature of water, a scientist must observe the experiment and write down important information. Recorded observations and measurements are called **data.** In this experiment, the data would include the time intervals at which the containers were observed, the temperatures of the water at each interval, and whether the water in either container was frozen or not. In most cases the data would be recorded in data tables such as those shown in Figure 1–12.

Data tables are a simple, organized way of recording information from an experiment. Sometimes, however, it is useful to visually compare the data. To do so, a scientist might construct a graph on which to plot the data. Because the data tables have two different types of measurements (time and temperature), the graph would have two axes. See Figure 1–13.

The horizontal axis of the graph would stand for the time measurements in the data tables. Time measurements were made every 5 minutes. So the horizontal axis would be marked with intervals of 5 minutes. The space between equal intervals would have to be equal. For example, the space between 10 minutes and 15 minutes would be the same as the space between 20 minutes and 25 minutes.

The vertical axis of the graph would stand for the temperature measurements in the data tables. The starting temperature of the water in the experiment was 25°C. The lowest temperature reached in the

Figure 1–12 *Scientists often record their observations in data tables. According to these data tables, at what temperature did the experiment begin? At what time intervals were the temperature measurements taken?*

WATER (Control setup)							
Time (min)	0	5	10	15	20	25	30
Temperature (°C)	25	20	15	10	5	0*	−10

* Asterisk means liquid has frozen.

WATER WITH SALT (experimental setup)							
Time (min)	0	5	10	15	20	25	30
Temperature (°C)	25	20	15	10	5	0	−10*

experiment was −10°C. So the vertical axis would begin with 25°C and end at −10°C. Each interval of temperature would have to be equal to every other interval of temperature.

After the axes of the graph were set up, the scientist would first graph the data from the experimental setup. Each pair of data points from the data table would be marked on the graph. At 0 minutes, for example, the temperature was 25°C. So the scientist would place a dot where 0 minutes and 25°C intersect—in the lower left corner of the graph. The next pair of data points was for 5 minutes and 20°C. So the scientist would lightly draw a vertical line from the 5-minute interval of the horizontal axis and then a horizontal line from the 20°C interval of the vertical axis. The scientist would then put a dot at the place where the two lines intersected. This dot would represent the data points 5 minutes and 20°C. The scientist would continue to plot all of the data pairs from the data table in this manner.

When all of the data pairs were plotted, the scientist would draw a line through all the dots. This line would represent the graph of the experimental setup data. Then the scientist would follow the same procedure to graph the data pairs from the control setup. Figure 1–13 shows what the two lines would look like.

Figure 1–13 *The information in data tables can be visually presented in graphs. What conclusions can you draw from these graphs about the effect of salt on the freezing point of water?*

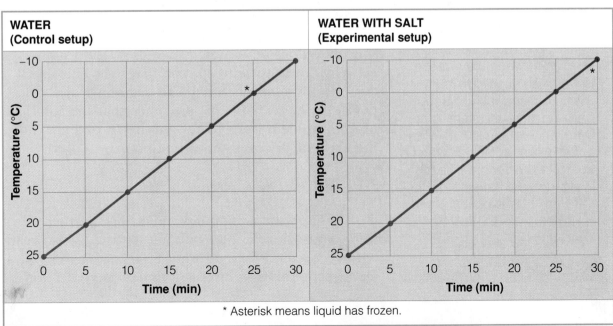

* Asterisk means liquid has frozen.

Figure 1–14 *Based on what you have learned, can you explain why mountain roads are often salted before a snowfall? What evidence do you have that this road was salted?*

The results from a single experiment are not enough to reach a conclusion. A scientist must run an experiment over and over again before the data can be considered accurate. From the data in this experiment, the scientist would quickly find that the temperatures in both containers fall at the same rate. But the fresh water freezes at a higher temperature than the salt water.

Stating a Conclusion

If the two friends walking along the beach had followed the same steps as a scientist, they would now be ready to state a conclusion. Their conclusion would be this: When salt is dissolved in water, the freezing temperature of the water goes down. For this reason, fresh water freezes at a higher temperature than does sea water.

Why does this happen, you may ask? This question sounds very much like the beginning of a new puzzle. It often happens in science that the solution of one problem leads to yet another problem. Thus the cycle of discovery goes on and on.

Repeating the Work

Although the two friends might be satisfied with their conclusion, not so with a scientist. As you read before, a scientist would want to repeat the experiment many times to be sure the data were accurate.

Activity DOING

Expanding Water?

Most substances on Earth contract, or become smaller in volume, when they freeze. Is water an exception? Using a small pan, water, and a freezing compartment, perform an experiment to discover whether or not water contracts when it freezes. Write down what you did in the form of a procedure and your results in the form of a conclusion.

So a scientific experiment must be able to be repeated. And before the conclusion of a scientist can be accepted by the scientific community, other scientists must repeat the experiment and check the results. So when a scientist writes a report on his or her experiment, that report must be detailed enough so that scientists throughout the world can repeat the experiment for themselves. In most cases, it is only when an experiment has been repeated by scientists worldwide is it considered to be accurate and worthy of being included in new scientific research.

PROBLEM ? ?? ? Solving

Fact or Fiction?

Perhaps one of the most interesting aspects of life science is the amazing variety of plants and animals living on planet Earth. Some of these organisms are so unusual that it is often difficult to determine if a statement is true or a figment of someone's imagination. Read the following hypothesis to see what we mean.

Hypothesis: Turtle eggs develop into male turtles in cold temperatures and into female turtles in warm temperatures.

Predict whether this hypothesis is fact or fiction. Then design a simple experiment to show if the hypothesis is or is not correct. Make sure your experiment has an experimental setup and a control setup.

The Scientific Method—Not Always So Orderly

By now it must seem as if science is a fairly predictable way of studying the world. After all, you state a problem, gather information, form a hypothesis, run an experiment, and determine a conclusion. It certainly sounds all neat and tidy. Well, sometimes it is—and sometimes it isn't!

In practice, scientists do not always follow all the steps in the scientific method. Nor do the steps always follow the same order. For example, while doing an experiment a scientist might observe something unusual or unexpected. That unexpected event might cause the scientist to discard the original hypothesis and suggest a new one. In this case, the hypothesis actually followed the experiment. In other cases, the problem to be studied might not be where the scientist begins. Let's go back to those unexpected results. Those results might cause the scientist to rethink the way she or he looks at the world. They might suggest new problems that need to be considered. In this case, the problem followed the experiment.

As you already learned, a good rule to follow is that all experiments should have only one variable. Sometimes, however, scientists run experiments with

Activity Bank

What Do Seeds Need to Grow?, p.102

Figure 1–15 *Why would it be difficult to study the effects of a single variable on these East African lions?*

Prefix	Meaning	Prefix	Meaning	Suffix	Meaning
anti-	against	herb-	pertaining to plants	-cyst	pouch
arth-	joint, jointed	hetero-	different	-derm	skin, layer
auto-	self	homeo-	same	-gen	producing
bio-	related to life	macro-	large	-itis	inflammation
chloro-	green	micro-	small	-logy	study
cyto-	cell	multi-	consisting of many units	-meter	measurement
di-	double	osteo-	bone	-osis	condition, disease
epi-	above	photo-	pertaining to light	-phage	eater
exo-	outer, external	plasm-	forming substance	-phase	stage
gastro-	stomach	proto-	first	-pod	foot
hemo-	blood	syn-	together	-stasis	stationary condition

Figure 1–16 *A working knowledge of prefixes and suffixes used in science vocabulary will be of great help to you. According to this chart, what is the meaning of the term arthropod?*

several variables. Naturally, the data in such experiments are much more difficult to analyze. For example, suppose scientists want to study lions in their natural environment in Africa. It is not likely they will be able to eliminate all the variables in the environment and concentrate on just a single one. So although a single variable is a good rule—and one that you will follow in almost all of the experiments you design or perform—it is not always practical in the real world.

There is yet another step in the scientific method that cannot always be followed. Believe it or not, many scientists search for the truths of nature without ever performing experiments. Sometimes the best they can rely on are observations and natural curiosity. Here's an example. Charles Darwin is considered the father of the theory of evolution (how living things change over time). Much of what we know about evolution is based on Darwin's work. Yet Darwin did not perform a single experiment! He based his hypotheses and theories on his observations of the natural world. Certainly it would have been better had Darwin performed experiments to prove his theory of evolution. But as the process of evolution generally takes thousands, even millions of years, performing an experiment would be a bit too time consuming!

ACTIVITY

THINKING

What's the Word?

Use the prefixes and suffixes in Figure 1–16 to determine the meanings of the following words:

biology gastritis
gastropod exoskeleton
photometer epidermis
homeostasis cytology

A Rocky Observation

To be useful, one person's observations must give meaningful information to another person.

1. Obtain four rocks of about equal size.

2. Place a small piece of masking tape on each rock and number the rocks 1 through 4.

3. On a sheet of paper, write down as many observations as you can about each rock next to its number.

4. Rewrite your observations without numbers on another sheet of paper. Give this sheet of paper and the rocks to a classmate.

5. Ask your classmate to match the observations to the rocks.

■ Did your classmate make correct matches? Why or why not?

The Scientific Method in Your World

A common question often asked by students is "Why are we studying science? What does it have to do with my world?" The answer is—plenty! Perhaps you have no real interest in the reason why fresh water freezes at a higher temperature than sea water. Maybe you live in a city or in a part of the country far removed from a beach. But regardless of where you live, people probably drive cars. And that means they may worry about the water in the car's radiator freezing in the winter and boiling over in the summer. How do we prevent these events from occurring? You probably know the answer—we add antifreeze to the radiator.

The principles behind the actions of antifreeze are exactly the same as the principles behind the fresh and salt water experiment. Adding antifreeze lowers the temperature at which the water freezes—an important point to know during the cold winter months. And, strangely enough, in much the same way antifreeze increases the boiling temperature of water so that cars are not as likely to overheat during the hot summer months.

You should keep this example in mind whenever you study science. For very often the concepts you are learning about have very practical applications in your world. When possible, we will point out the relevance of the material you are studying. But that may not always be practical. So it's up to you to remember that science is not just for laboratory workers in white coats. Science affects all of us— each and every day of our lives.

1–2 Section Review

1. List and describe the steps in the scientific method.

2. Explain the importance of running both an experimental setup and a control setup.

Connection—*You and Your World*

3. One morning you wake up and discover that your radio no longer works. How might you apply the steps of the scientific method to determine the cause of the problem?

Messages From Outer Space?

Have we been receiving radio messages from outer space? In 1933, people believed we were. They were wrong, but their mistake is an interesting example of how luck, or serendipity, plays a role in science and, in this case, can shake up society for a little while.

Here's how it all happened. In 1931, Bell Telephone scientists wanted to find out what was causing static on some radio telephone lines. The scientists suspected (hypothesized) that the static might be caused by thunderstorms. They asked a young scientist named Karl Jansky to see if he could find out whether this was true. Jansky built a special antenna to try to solve the problem. He mounted his antenna on some wheels from an old car so that he could aim the antenna at any part of the sky. Because it could be turned around, Jansky's invention was nicknamed "the merry-go-round."

Jansky found that almost all of the static was indeed caused by radio waves from thunderstorms. But his an-

tenna had also picked up a faint hissing sound that he could not explain. Jansky could have shrugged his shoulders and ignored this hissing sound, but his curiosity got the best of him. So he decided to investigate. He would try to track down the hissing sounds.

Jansky carried on observations for two years. Eventually, he found that the hiss moved across the sky, as did the stars. In 1933, Jansky announced that the radio waves producing the hissing sound were actually coming to Earth from outer space! Jansky's discovery that radio waves were coming from space became an overnight sensation. Newspaper headlines throughout the world reported the finding. But after only a few weeks, most people seemed to forget Jansky's discovery.

Then, in 1937, an amateur radio operator named Grote Reber had a hunch that Jansky's discovery was important. So Reber built a 10-meter dish antenna in his backyard to capture the radio waves from space. This instrument became the world's first radio telescope. Jansky's unexpected discovery and Reber's hunch gave astronomers a new way of exploring the sky. The science of *radio astronomy,* which would produce many exciting discoveries of its own, had been born.

1–3 Science and Discovery

Scientific discoveries are not always made by following the scientific method. **Sometimes a discovery is made because of luck, a hunch, or a new way of looking at (observing) the world.** Remember, the most important trait of any scientist is curiosity. And some of the greatest sparks of curiosity have been experienced when they were least expected.

Recently, two American biologists, Dr. Patricia Bonamo and Dr. James Grierson, discovered a special group of fossils. Fossils are the remains of organisms that lived in the past. While looking for extinct plant specimens in rocks from northern New York, these scientists found something different and unexpected. Instead of plant fossils, the scientists discovered fossils of some of the first land animals. Fossilized centipedes, shells and claws of spiderlike creatures, and a single mite were discovered.

There was much that was amazing about this discovery. The centipede, only 2.54 centimeters long, had its many pairs of legs well preserved. The sense organs of several of the spiderlike creatures were easily recognizable.

Scientists described the fossils as looking as though "they might have died yesterday." But these organisms had not died "yesterday," and that was the most amazing discovery of all. Tests showed that the animals had died about 380 million years ago! Until this discovery, the earliest totally land-living

Figure 1–17 *An artist's concept of what Earth's forests looked like some 350 million years ago.*

animals ever discovered had been 300 million years old. Drs. Bonamo and Grierson had turned back the birthday of such animals by 80 million years.

"When we first saw the animals in our samples, we thought they might have fallen in by accident, from the light fixtures or cracks in the wall. But one spiderlike animal had its legs still embedded in the rock." This statement by Drs. Bonamo and Grierson shows how their fossil discovery was an exciting piece of good luck. But it is also an example of scientists recognizing something special when they see it.

1–3 Section Review

1. The term serendipity means making a fortunate discovery through an accident. What role does serendipity play in science?

Critical Thinking—*Making Generalizations*
2. What does this fossil discovery indicate about the appearance of land-living animals?

An Unexpected World

You would be amazed at the microscopic creatures that share your home with you. If you are interested in these strange organisms, read *The Secret House*, by David Bodanis. You will never look at your room in quite the same way again!

1–4 Safety in the Science Laboratory

The scientific laboratory is a place of adventure and discovery. Some of the most exciting events in scientific history have happened in the laboratory. For example, the structure of DNA, the blueprint of life, was discovered by scientists in the laboratory. The plastics used today for clothing and other products were first made by scientists in a laboratory. And the laboratory was where scientists discovered the relationship between electricity and magnetism. The list goes on and on.

To better understand the concepts you will read about in science, it is likely you will work in the laboratory too. If you follow instructions and are as careful as a scientist would be, the laboratory will turn out to be an exciting experience for you.

Scientists know that when working in the laboratory, it is very important to follow safety procedures.

Guide for Reading

Focus on this question as you read.

▶ *What important safety rules must you follow when working in the laboratory?*

Figure 1–18 *It is important to always point a test tube that is being heated away from yourself and your classmates (right). What two safety precautions is this student taking before picking up a hot beaker (left)?*

The most important safety rule is to always follow your teacher's directions or the directions in your textbook exactly as stated. You should never try anything on your own without asking your teacher first. And when you are not sure what you should do, always ask first.

As you read the laboratory investigations in your textbook, you will see safety alert symbols. These symbols indicate that special safety precautions must be taken. Look at Figure 1–19 to learn the meanings of these safety symbols and the important safety procedures you should take.

In addition to the safety procedures listed in Figure 1–19, there is a more detailed list of safety procedures in Appendix B on page 112 at the back of this textbook. Before you enter the laboratory for the first time, make sure you have read each rule carefully. Then read all the rules over again, making sure you understand each rule. If you do not understand a rule, ask your teacher to explain it. You may even want to suggest further rules that apply to your particular classroom.

1–4 Section Review

1. What is the most important general rule to follow when working in the laboratory?
2. Suppose your teacher asks you to boil some water in a test tube. What precautions should you take to make sure this activity is done safely?

Connection—*You and Your World*

3. How can you apply the safety rules in Figure 1–19 to rules that should be followed when working in a kitchen? In a machine shop?

Glassware Safety

1. Whenever you see this symbol, you will know that you are working with glassware that can easily be broken. Take particular care to handle such glassware safely. And never use broken or chipped glassware.
2. Never heat glassware that is not thoroughly dry. Never pick up any glassware unless you are sure it is not hot. If it is hot, use heat-resistant gloves.
3. Always clean glassware thoroughly before putting it away.

Fire Safety

1. Whenever you see this symbol, you will know that you are working with fire. Never use any source of fire without wearing safety goggles.
2. Never heat anything—particularly chemicals—unless instructed to do so.
3. Never heat anything in a closed container.
4. Never reach across a flame.
5. Always use a clamp, tongs, or heat-resistant gloves to handle hot objects.
6. Always maintain a clean work area, particularly when using a flame.

Heat Safety

Whenever you see this symbol, you will know that you should put on heat-resistant gloves to avoid burning your hands.

Chemical Safety

1. Whenever you see this symbol, you will know that you are working with chemicals that could be hazardous.
2. Never smell any chemical directly from its container. Always use your hand to waft some of the odors from the top of the container toward your nose—and only when instructed to do so.
3. Never mix chemicals unless instructed to do so.
4. Never touch or taste any chemical unless instructed to do so.
5. Keep all lids closed when chemicals are not in use. Dispose of all chemicals as instructed by your teacher.

6. Immediately rinse with water any chemicals, particularly acids, that get on your skin and clothes. Then notify your teacher.

Eye and Face Safety

1. Whenever you see this symbol, you will know that you are performing an experiment in which you must take precautions to protect your eyes and face by wearing safety goggles.
2. When you are heating a test tube or bottle, always point it away from you and others. Chemicals can splash or boil out of a heated test tube.

Sharp Instrument Safety

1. Whenever you see this symbol, you will know that you are working with a sharp instrument.
2. Always use single-edged razors; double-edged razors are too dangerous.
3. Handle any sharp instrument with extreme care. Never cut any material toward you; always cut away from you.
4. Immediately notify your teacher if your skin is cut.

Electrical Safety

1. Whenever you see this symbol, you will know that you are using electricity in the laboratory.
2. Never use long extension cords to plug in any electrical device. Do not plug too many appliances into one socket or you may overload the socket and cause a fire.
3. Never touch an electrical appliance or outlet with wet hands.

Animal Safety

1. Whenever you see this symbol, you will know that you are working with live animals.
2. Do not cause pain, discomfort, or injury to an animal.
3. Follow your teacher's directions when handling animals. Wash your hands thoroughly after handling animals or their cages.

Figure 1–19 *You should become familiar with these safety symbols because you will see them in the laboratory investigations in this textbook.*

Laboratory Investigation

A Moldy Question

Problem

What variables affect the growth of bread mold?

Materials *(per group)*

2 jars with lids
2 slices of bread
1 medicine dropper

Procedure ⚗

1. Put half a slice of bread into each jar. Moisten each half slice with ten drops of water. Cap the jars tightly. Keep one jar in sunlight and place the other in a dark closet.

2. Observe the jars every few days for about two weeks. Record your observations. Does light seem to influence mold growth? Include your answer to this question (your conclusion) with your observations.

3. Ask your teacher what scientists know about the effect of light on mold growth. Was your conclusion correct? Think again: What other variables might have affected mold growth? Did you think of temperature? How about moisture? Light, temperature, and moisture are all possible variables in this investigation.

4. Design a second experiment to retest the effect of light on mold growth. Record your procedure, observations, and conclusions.

5. Design another experiment to test one of the other variables. Test only one variable at a time. Work with other groups of students in your class so that each group tests one of the other two variables. Share your results and draw your conclusions together.

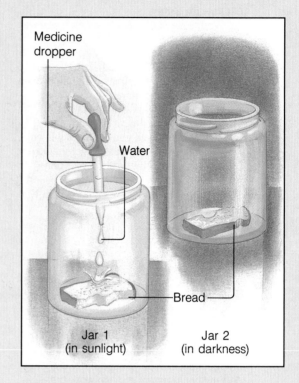

Jar 1
(in sunlight)

Jar 2
(in darkness)

Observations

Study the class data for this experiment. What variables seem to affect mold growth?

Analysis and Conclusions

1. In each of your additional experiments, what variable were you testing? Did you have a control setup for each experiment? If so, describe it.

2. Juanita set up the following experiment: She placed a piece of orange peel in each of two jars. She added 3 milliliters of water to jar 1 and placed it in the refrigerator. She added no water to jar 2 and placed it on a windowsill in the kitchen. At the end of a week, she noticed more mold growth in jar 2. Juanita concluded that light, a warm temperature, and no moisture are ideal conditions for mold growth. Discuss the accuracy of Juanita's conclusion.

Summarizing Key Concepts

1–1 Science—Not Just for Scientists

▲ The goal of science is to understand the world around us.

▲ Scientists use facts as clues to the large mysteries of nature.

▲ A theory is the most logical explanation for events that occur in nature. A theory is a time-tested concept that makes useful and dependable predictions about the natural world.

▲ The three main branches of science are life science, earth science, and physical science.

▲ Life scientists study living things and their parts and actions.

▲ Earth scientists study the features of the Earth, which include rocks, oceans, volcanoes, earthquakes, and the atmosphere. Astronomy, which is a part of earth science, is the study of objects such as stars, planets, and moons.

▲ Physical scientists study matter and energy. Physical science can be further divided into chemistry and physics. The study of substances and how they change and combine is the focus of chemistry. The study of energy is the focus of physics.

▲ Within any branch of science, most scientists specialize in a particular area of study.

1–2 The Scientific Method—A Way of Problem Solving

▲ The scientific method is the systematic way of problem solving used by scientists.

▲ The basic steps in the scientific method are stating the problem, gathering information, forming a hypothesis, experimenting, recording and analyzing data, stating a conclusion, and repeating the work.

▲ A hypothesis is a proposed solution to a scientific problem.

▲ A variable is the one factor that is being tested in an experiment.

▲ Scientists run an experimental setup and a control setup, or experiment without the variable, to make sure the results of the experiment were caused by the variable and not some hidden factor.

1–3 Science and Discovery

▲ Not all scientific discoveries are made through the scientific method. Sometimes luck or a hunch leads to an important discovery.

1–4 Safety in the Science Laboratory

▲ When working in the laboratory, it is important to heed all necessary safety precautions. These include using safety equipment and following all instructions carefully.

Reviewing Key Terms

Define each term in a complete sentence.

1–1 Science—Not Just for Scientists
theory
law

1–2 The Scientific Method—A Way of Problem Solving
scientific method
hypothesis
variable
control
data

Chapter Review

Content Review

Multiple Choice

Choose the letter of the answer that best completes each statement.

1. An orderly, systematic approach to problem solving is called the
   a. experiment.
   b. conclusion.
   c. hypothesis.
   d. scientific method.
2. The factor being tested in an experiment is the
   a. hypothesis.   c. control.
   b. variable.   d. problem.
3. Recorded observations and measurements are called
   a. data.   c. conclusions.
   b. graphs.   d. variables.
4. The most important laboratory safety rule is to
   a. have a partner.
   b. wear a lab coat.
   c. wear safety goggles.
   d. always follow directions.
5. The branch of science that deals with the study of ocean currents is
   a. life science.   c. earth science.
   b. chemistry.   d. physics.
6. Scientists must analyze the results of an experiment before they form a
   a. hypothesis.   c. data table.
   b. conclusion.   d. variable.
7. A time-tested concept that makes useful and dependable predictions about the world is called a(an)
   a. hypothesis.   c. theory.
   b. discovery.   d. investigation.
8. A safety symbol in the shape of a flask alerts you to
   a. be careful with lab animals.
   b. be careful with glassware.
   c. wear safety goggles.
   d. wear heat-resistant gloves.

True or False

If the statement is true, write "true." If it is false, change the underlined word or words to make the statement true.

1. Never heat anything in an <u>open</u> container.
2. Recorded observations that often involve measurements are called <u>conclusions</u>.
3. The part of the experiment with the variable is called the <u>experimental setup</u>.
4. The <u>scientific method</u> is a proposed solution to a scientific problem.
5. Most experiments must have <u>two</u> <u>variables</u> to be accurate.
6. The study of heat and light is part of <u>physics</u>.
7. The symbol of a <u>razor blade</u> means you are working with a sharp instrument.

Concept Mapping

Complete the following concept map for Section 1–1. Refer to pages A6–A7 to construct a concept map for the entire chapter.

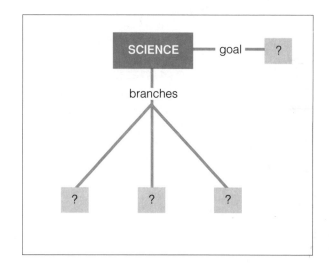

Concept Mastery

Discuss each of the following in a brief paragraph.

1. Why should an experiment contain only one variable? What is the purpose of the control in an experiment?
2. List and describe at least three examples of how you act like a scientist.
3. Why are some problems in science impossible to study through laboratory experimentation?
4. Describe the basic steps of the scientific method.
5. What role can luck or chance play in the advancement of science?
6. Describe three science questions that you have an interest in finding an answer to.

Critical Thinking and Problem Solving

Use the skills you have developed in this chapter to answer each of the following.

1. **Following safety rules** Explain the potential danger involved in each of the following situations. Describe the safety precautions that should be used to avoid injury to you or your classmates.
   a. Pushing a rubber stopper far down into a test tube
   b. Pouring acid into a beaker while sitting at your lab table
   c. Tasting a white powder to see if it is salty
   d. Heating a stoppered test tube of water
   e. Deciding on your own to mix two chemicals together
2. **Applying concepts** Explain how the scientific method could be used by a mechanic to determine why a car won't start on a cold morning.
3. **Designing an experiment** The following hypothesis is suggested to you: Water will heat up faster when placed under the direct rays of the sun than when placed under indirect, or angled, rays of the sun. Design an experiment to test this hypothesis. Make sure you have both a variable and a control setup. With your teacher's permission, conduct the experiment and draw a conclusion about the hypothesis.
4. **Making predictions** Develop a time line in which you predict some of the major advances in science during the twenty-first century.
5. **Making charts** Construct a picture chart that shows the fields of study included in the three main branches of science.
6. **Designing an experiment** Design an experiment to determine the best place to grow flowers in your classroom. With your teacher's permission, conduct the experiment and draw a conclusion.
7. **Using the writing process** Write a short story that begins, "It was a dark and eerie night. As the lost hikers knocked on the door of the scientist's laboratory, they suddenly realized . . ."

Measurement and the Sciences

Slowly, ever so carefully, the robot arm of the *Space Shuttle Discovery* released the *Hubble Space Telescope* into orbit above the Earth on April 25, 1990. The *Hubble Space Telescope* had been more than a decade in the making at a cost of several billion dollars. The 2.4-meter primary mirror was the most carefully constructed and most expensive mirror ever built. The development of the primary mirror was a monumental scientific achievement—or was it?

Soon after its launch, scientists discovered a problem with the primary mirror. Light striking the outer edge of the mirror was brought to a focus about 4 centimeters behind light striking the center of the mirror. As a result, the images produced by the telescope were fuzzy and not as clear as expected. A slight miscalculation in measurement had been built into the mirror's design.

The *Hubble Space Telescope* will be repaired. In time it will bring us pictures of the universe we can only dream about today. But until that day, it stands as a reminder to all scientists—and those who would be scientists—that careful and precise measurements can be the difference between scientific success and failure.

Journal *Activity*

You and Your World Pick a type of measurement. Perhaps length is your favorite. Or you may prefer temperature or volume. Whatever type of measurement you choose, make an entry in your journal each time you use that type of measurement on a particular day.

The Hubble Space Telescope *being released by the robot arm on the* Space Shuttle Discovery.

Guide for Reading

Focus on this question as you read.

▶ What are the basic units of measurement in the metric system?

Create a Measurement System

Using objects found in your classroom as standards, create your own measurement system for length, mass, and volume. For each type of measurement, try to include units of several different sizes. Keep in mind that your ''standards'' must be things that will remain constant over time. Also keep in mind that you should be able to convert easily from one unit to another.

Once your measurement system is established, create a display of your standard objects and the units they represent. Then challenge members of your class to use your system to make measurements of various objects and distances.

2–1 The Metric System

*Magnum est ut inter sese colloqui
possint periti in scientiae rebus.*

Having trouble reading the sentence written above? Don't worry, it's not a string of new vocabulary words you have to memorize. Actually, it is a very clear and concise sentence. It just happens to be written in a language you probably don't understand. And it's been included to make a simple but important point. Science is a worldwide topic, and scientists come from every country on Earth. If they are to work together and know what each other is doing, scientists must be able to communicate—in a sense, to speak the same language. In case you're wondering, the sentence above is in Latin. Its translation is:

*It is important that scientists can
communicate with each other.*

Metrics—The Universal Language of Measurement

In Chapter 1 you learned that experiments are an important part of the scientific method. You also learned that most experiments require data in the form of measurements. It is important that measurements be accurate and easily communicated to other people. So a universal system of measurement having standard units must be used. You can imagine the confusion that would result if measurements were made without standard units. For example, suppose you ask a friend how far it is to his house, and his response is five. You do not know if he means five blocks, five kilometers, or that it takes about five minutes to get there. Obviously, such a response would be of little help to you—and you probably would not accept that answer.

Scientists are ordinary people just like you. In order to make sure there is little confusion about their work, all scientists use the same standard system of measurement. The scientific system of measurement is called the **metric system.** The metric system is often referred to as the International System

COMMON METRIC UNITS

Length	Mass
1 meter (m) = 100 centimeters (cm) 1 meter = 1000 millimeters (mm) 1 meter = 1,000,000 micrometers (µm) 1 meter = 1,000,000,000 nanometers (nm) 1 meter = 10,000,000,000 angstroms (Å) 1000 meters = 1 kilometer (km)	1 kilogram (kg) = 1000 grams (g) 1 gram = 1000 milligrams (mg) 1000 kilograms = 1 metric ton (t)
Volume	**Temperature**
1 liter (L) = 1000 milliliters (mL) or 1000 cubic centimeters (cm³)	0°C = freezing point of water 100°C = boiling point of water
kilo- = one thousand centi- = one hundredth milli- = one thousandth	micro- = one millionth nano- = one billionth

of Units, or SI. Using the metric system, scientists all over the world can compare and analyze their data.

The metric system is a simple system to use. Like our money system, the metric system is a decimal system; that is, it is based on the number ten and multiples of ten. (There are ten pennies in a dime, ten dimes in a dollar, and so on.) In much the same way, each unit in the metric system is ten times larger or ten times smaller than the next smaller or larger unit. So calculations with metric units are relatively easy.

Scientists use metric units to measure length, volume, mass, weight, density, and temperature. Some frequently used metric units and their abbreviations are listed in Figure 2–1.

Length

The basic unit of length in the metric system is the **meter** (m). A meter is equal to 39.4 inches, or a little more than a yard. Your height would be measured in meters. Most students your age are between 1.5 and 2 meters tall.

To measure the length of an object smaller than a meter, scientists use the metric unit called the **centimeter** (cm). The prefix *centi-* means one-hundredth. As you might guess, there are 100 centimeters in a meter. The height of this book is about 26 centimeters.

Figure 2–1 *The metric system is easy to use because it is based on units of ten. How many centimeters are there in 10 meters?*

ACTIVITY
DISCOVERING

Charting Growth

Make a height recorder in your classroom. Place a meterstick vertically 1 meter above the floor. Use transparent tape to secure the meterstick to the wall. Measure your height using the meterstick. Measure the heights of your classmates in the same way. Do not forget to add 100 cm (1 m) to every measurement you take! Keep growth records for each member of the class for the duration of the school year. Keep in mind that everyone grows at a different rate.

■ At the end of the year, calculate the growth of each student. Add up the total growth of the class in centimeters. Are you impressed?

Figure 2-2 *Which metric unit of length would be most appropriate when measuring the height of the Matterhorn in Switzerland or giraffes in Kenya?*

To measure even smaller objects, the metric unit called the **millimeter** (mm) is used. The prefix *milli-* means one-thousandth. So there are 1000 millimeters in a meter. In bright light, the diameter of the pupil of your eye is about 1 millimeter. How many millimeters are there in a centimeter?

Even millimeters are too large to use when describing the sizes of microscopic organisms such as bacteria. Bacteria are measured in micrometers, or millionths of a meter, and nanometers, or billionths of a meter. That may seem small enough for any measurement, but it's not. To describe the size of

Figure 2-3 *The length of bacteria (right) are measured in micrometers or nanometers. What unit of length is used when measuring atoms such as these silicon atoms (left)?*

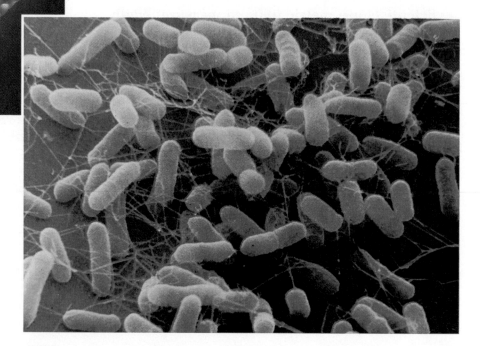

Figure 2–4 *To measure the length of long rivers, scientists would choose the unit of length called the kilometer.*

atoms, the building blocks of matter, scientists use the metric unit called the angstrom. An angstrom is equal to one ten-billionth of a meter!

Sometimes scientists need to measure large distances, such as the length of the Nile River in Africa. Such lengths can be measured in meters, centimeters, or even millimeters. But when measuring large distances with small units, the numbers become very difficult to work with. For example, the length of the Nile River is about 6,649,000,000 millimeters—not an easy number to use! To avoid such large numbers, scientists use the metric unit called the **kilometer** (km). The prefix *kilo-* means one thousand. So there are 1000 meters in a kilometer. The length of the Nile River is about 6649 kilometers. How many meters is this?

On Earth, meters and kilometers are very useful units of measurement. But in space, distances are often too great to be measured in kilometers. (Again, the numbers start getting very large.) To measure long distances in space, astronomers use a unit of distance called the **light-year.** A light-year is the distance light travels in one year. As you probably know, light travels mighty fast—about 300,000 kilometers per second. A light-year, then, is about 9.5 trillion kilometers. No, we won't ask you how many millimeters are in a light-year, but you might have fun figuring it out on your own. You can think of a light-year as a ruler made of light. But keep in mind that a light-year measures distance, not time.

A light-year may seem like an enormous distance, but in space, it is not very far at all. The closest star system to the Earth is over 4 light-years away. It takes the light from that star system over four years to reach the Earth. Yet even that distance seems quite short when compared to the distance of the farthest known star system, which is about 12 billion light-years away. The light from these most distant stars may take more than 12 billion years to reach Earth. Unbelieveable as it may seem, the light began its long journey toward Earth before the Earth had even formed.

Figure 2–5 *What unit of length is used to measure distant objects in space, such as this galaxy?*

Volume

Volume is the amount of space an object takes up. In the metric system, the basic unit of volume is the **liter** (L). A liter is slightly larger than a quart. To measure volumes smaller than a liter, scientists use the **milliliter** (mL). Recall that the prefix *milli-* means one-thousandth. So there are 1000 milliliters in a liter. An ordinary drinking glass holds about 200 milliliters of liquid. How many milliliters are there in 10 liters?

Liters and milliliters are used to measure the volume of liquids. Of course, both you and scientists may need to measure the volume of solids as well. The metric unit used to measure the volume of solids is called the **cubic centimeter** (cm³ or cc). A cubic centimeter is equal to the volume of a cube that measures 1 centimeter by 1 centimeter by 1 centimeter. It just so happens that a cubic centimeter is exactly equal in volume to a milliliter. (We told you the metric system is easy to use.) In fact, cubic centimeters can be used to measure the volume of liquids as well as solids. How many cubic centimeters are there in a liter?

Figure 2–6 *A cubic centimeter (cm³ or cc) is the volume of a cube that measures 1 cm by 1 cm by 1 cm. How many milliliters are in a cubic centimeter?*

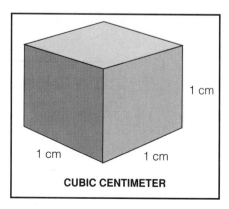

1 cm

1 cm   1 cm

CUBIC CENTIMETER

Figure 2–7 *To measure the volume of water rushing over Iguazu Falls in Brazil, scientists would use the unit of volume called the liter. What unit of volume would they use to measure the amount of water in a pet's water dish?*

Mass

Mass is a measure of the amount of matter in an object. For example, there is more matter in a dumptruck than in a mid-sized car. So a dumptruck has more mass than a mid-sized car. Which has more mass, a mid-sized car or a bicycle?

Keep in mind that mass is different from volume. Volume is the amount of space an object takes up, whereas mass is the amount of matter in the object. The basic unit of mass in the metric system is the **kilogram** (kg).

The kilogram is a useful unit when measuring the mass of large objects. To measure the mass of small objects, such as a nickel, the **gram** (g) is used. If you remember what the prefix *kilo-* means, then you know that a kilogram contains 1000 grams. A nickel has a mass of about 5 grams. How many grams are in 20 kilograms?

ACTIVITY

DISCOVERING

A Milliliter by Any Other Name

■ Use a graduated cylinder, water, a metric ruler, and a small rectangular solid made of a material that sinks in water to prove that 1 milliliter = 1 cubic centimeter.

Figure 2–8 *The buffalo is one of the largest land animals on Earth. Harvest field mice are the smallest mice on Earth. Which metric unit would be best for measuring the mass of the buffalo? Of field mice?*

As you might expect, scientists often need to measure the mass of objects much smaller than a nickel. To do so, they use the metric unit called the **milligram** (mg). Again, recall that the prefix *milli-* means one-thousandth. So there are 1000 milligrams in a gram. How many milligrams are there in a kilogram?

Weight

Weight is a measure of the attraction between two objects due to gravity. Gravity is a force of attraction. The strength of the gravitational force between objects depends in part on the distance between these objects. As the distance between objects becomes greater, the gravitational force between the objects decreases. On Earth, your weight is a measure of the Earth's force of gravity on you.

The basic unit of weight in the metric system is the **newton** (N), named after Isaac Newton who discovered the force of gravity. The newton is used because it is a measure of force, and weight is the amount of force the Earth's gravity exerts on an object. An object with a mass of 1 kilogram is pulled toward the Earth with a force of 9.8 newtons. So the weight of the object is 9.8 N. An object with a mass of 50 kilograms is pulled toward the Earth with a force of 50 × 9.8, or 490 N. That object's weight is 490 N. What is your weight on Earth?

Because the force of gravity changes with distance, your weight can change depending on your location. For example, you are farther from the center of the Earth when standing atop a tall mountain than when standing at sea level. And although the change may be small, you actually weigh less at the top of the mountain than you do at sea level. How might your weight change if you went down into a deep mine?

We often describe astronauts orbiting above the Earth as being weightless. You now know that this description is not correct. The distance between the astronauts and the center of the Earth is so great that the Earth's gravitational force is less strong. The astronauts appear to be weightless, but they actually are not. They still have weight because they

Figure 2–9 *Although we speak of astronauts as being "weightless," they are not. However, on Earth this astronaut would never have been able to lift this heavy communications satellite. But he was able to lift it with ease while floating above the Earth. Can you explain why?*

ACTIVITY

DISCOVERING

Does Air Have Mass and Weight?

1. Blow up two balloons to an equal size.

2. Tape or tie each balloon to one end of a meterstick.

3. Attach a string to the center of the meterstick. Hold the string so that the balloons are balanced. If the balloons are of equal size, the meterstick will be horizontal to the floor.

4. Carefully burst one of the balloons with a pin. What happens?

■ Use the results of your experiment to determine if air has mass, weight, or both.

Figure 2–10 *The mass of planet Neptune is much greater than that of Earth, while the moon's mass is only about one sixth that of Earth. How would your weight on Neptune compare with your weight on Earth? On the moon? Is the same true of your mass?*

Calculating Density, p.104

are still being pulled toward the Earth by the force of gravity.

As you just read, the strength of the gravitational force changes with distance. But it also changes depending on mass. An object with a large mass, such as the Earth, exerts a strong gravitational force on other objects. (Which is why you remain rooted to the ground and don't float off into space.) But any object with mass exerts a gravitational force— and that includes you! There is actually a gravitational force of attraction between you and this textbook. But don't worry, the book will not come flying at you as a result of gravity. Why? Your mass is much too small.

We tend to think of the Earth as being extremely large. But as objects in space go, the Earth is not so big. The mass of the planet Jupiter is more than two and one-half times that of Earth. If you could stand on Jupiter, you would find that your weight would be two and one-half times greater than your weight on Earth. The mass of the moon is about one sixth that of the Earth. How would your weight on the moon compare with your weight on Earth?

It should be clear to you by now that mass remains a constant, but weight can change. The amount of matter in an object does not change regardless of where the object is located. But the weight of an object can change due to its location.

Density

Sometimes scientists need to compare substances based on their mass and volume. The relationship between mass and volume is called **density.**

Density is defined as the mass per unit volume of a substance. That may sound complicated, but it really isn't. Perhaps the following formula, which shows the relationship between density, mass, and volume, will help:

$$\text{Density} = \frac{\text{Mass}}{\text{Volume}}$$

Suppose a substance has a mass of 10 grams and a volume of 10 milliliters. If you divide the mass of

10 grams by the volume of 10 milliliters, you obtain the density of the substance:

$$\frac{10 \text{ g}}{10 \text{ mL}} = \frac{1 \text{ g}}{\text{mL}}$$

As it turns out, this substance is water. The density of water is 1 g/mL. Objects with a density less than that of water will float on water. Objects with a density greater than that of water will sink. Does iron have a density less than or greater than 1 g/mL?

Temperature

In the metric system, temperature is measured on the **Celsius** scale. On this temperature scale, water freezes at 0°C and boils at 100°C. This is not an accident. The metric system of temperature was set up in such a way that there are exactly 100 degrees between the freezing point and boiling point of water. (Remember the metric system is based on units of 10.) Normal body temperature is 37°C. Comfortable room temperature is about 21°C.

Dimensional Analysis

You now know the basic units of measurement in the metric system. But there is still one more thing you must learn—how to go from one unit to another. The skill of converting one unit to another is called **dimensional analysis.** Dimensional analysis involves determining in what units a problem is

Figure 2–11 *To increase her density so that she can sink to the depths of the sea bottom, this scuba diver wears a belt of lead weights.*

Activity Bank
Dazzling Displays of Densities, p.106

Figure 2–12 *You can see by the way this lizard walks lightly across the hot desert sands that temperature has an effect on almost all living things. Scientists measure temperature in degrees Celsius.*

given, in what units the answer should be, and the factor to be used to make the conversion from one unit to another. Keep in mind that you can only convert units that measure the same thing. That is, no matter how hard you try, you cannot convert length in kilometers to temperature in degrees Celsius.

To perform dimensional analysis, you must use a **conversion factor.** A conversion factor is a fraction that *always* equals 1. For example, 1 kilometer equals 1000 meters. So the fraction 1 kilometer/ 1000 meters equals 1. You can flip the conversion factor and it still equals 1: 1000 meters/1 kilometer equals 1.

In any fraction, the top number is called the numerator. The bottom number is called the denominator. So in a conversion fraction the numerator always equals the denominator and the fraction always equals 1.

This is probably beginning to sound a lot more complicated than it actually is. Let's see how it all works by using an example. Suppose you are told to convert 7500 grams to kilograms. This means that grams are your given unit and you are to convert grams to kilograms. (Your answer must be expressed in kilograms.) The conversion factor you choose must contain the relationship between grams and kilograms that has a value of 1. You have two possible choices:

$$\frac{1000 \text{ grams}}{1 \text{ kilogram}} = 1 \quad \text{or} \quad \frac{1 \text{ kilogram}}{1000 \text{ grams}} = 1$$

To convert one metric unit to another, you must multiply the given quantity times the conversion factor. Remember that multiplying a number by 1 does not change the value of the number. So multiplying by a conversion factor does not change the value of the quantity, only its units.

Now, which conversion factor should you use to change 7500 grams to kilograms? Since you want the given unit to cancel out during multiplication, you should use the conversion whose denominator has the same units as the units you wish to convert. Because you are converting grams into kilograms, the denominator of the conversion factor you use must be in grams and the numerator in kilograms.

The first step in dimensional analysis, then, is to write out the given quantity, the correct conversion factor, and a multiplication symbol between them:

$$7500 \text{ grams} \times \frac{1 \text{ kilogram}}{1000 \text{ grams}}$$

The next step is to cancel out the same units:

$$7500 \text{ grams} \times \frac{1 \text{ kilogram}}{1000 \text{ grams}}$$

The last step is to multiply:

$$7500 \times \frac{1 \text{ kilogram}}{1000} = \frac{7500 \text{ kilograms}}{1000}$$

$$\frac{7500 \text{ kilograms}}{1000} = 7.5 \text{ kilograms}$$

PROBLEM Solving

Dimension Convention

You have been selected as your school's representative to the International Dimension Convention. The purpose of the convention is to select the dimensional analysis champion. In order to help you bring home the trophy, your classmates have developed the following problems for you to solve. Keep in mind that the champion will be determined on both speed and accuracy.

Making Conversions

1. Two friends are training for the track team. One friend runs 5000 meters each morning. The other friend runs about 3 kilometers. Which friend is training the hardest?

2. Data from several experiments have been sent to you for analysis. To compare the data, however, you must convert the following measurements to the same units.

20 kilograms
700 grams
0.004 kilograms
300 milligrams

3. Your cat's bowl holds 0.25 liter. You have about 300 cubic centimeters of milk. Will all the milk fit in the bowl?

4. A recipe calls for 350 grams of flour. You have used 0.4 kilogram. Did you put in too much, too little, or just the right amount?

2-1 Section Review

1. What are the basic units of length, volume, mass, weight, and temperature in the metric system?
2. Compare mass and weight.
3. On what scale is temperature measured in the metric system? What are the fixed points on this scale?
4. What metric unit of length would be appropriate for measuring the distance from the Earth to the sun? Why?

Critical Thinking—*Applying Concepts*
5. Without placing an object in water, how can you determine if it will float?

Guide for Reading

Focus on this question as you read.

▶ *What laboratory tools are used to measure length, mass, volume, and temperature?*

2-2 Measurement Tools

Scientists use a wide variety of tools in order to study the world around them. Some of these tools are rather complex; others are relatively simple. In Chapter 3 you will discover more about the specific tools used by Life scientists, Earth scientists, and Physical scientists.

Because all sciences involve measurement, there are certain tools of measurement used by all scientists. You too will have an opportunity to use these tools when you perform activities and laboratory investigations. **The basic laboratory tools that you will learn to use are the metric ruler, triple-beam balance, graduated cylinder, and Celsius thermometer.**

Measuring Length

The most common tool used to measure length is the metric ruler. A metric ruler is divided into centimeters. Most metric rulers are between 15 and 30 centimeters in length. Each centimeter is further divided into 10 millimeters. Figure 2–13 shows a

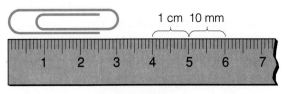

METRIC RULER

Figure 2–13 *A metric ruler is used to measure the length of small objects. What is the length of this paper clip?*

metric ruler and the centimeter and millimeter divisions.

Sometimes you will need to measure objects longer than a metric ruler. To do so, you can use a meterstick. A meterstick is 1 meter long. So there are 100 centimeters in a meterstick. How many millimeters will be marked on a meterstick? Why won't you find angstroms marked off on a meterstick?

Measuring Mass

As you just learned, the kilogram is the basic unit of mass in the metric system. A kilogram is equal to 1000 grams. Most of the measurements you will make in science will be in grams. The most common tool used to measure mass is the triple-beam balance. See Figure 2–14.

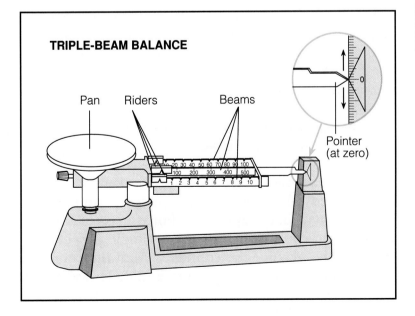

TRIPLE-BEAM BALANCE

Pan   Riders   Beams

Pointer
(at zero)

Metric Measurements

Here are some measurements you can make about yourself and your surroundings. Use the metric units of length, mass, volume, and temperature. Record your measurements on a chart.

Make the following measurements about yourself:
  a. Height
  b. Arm length
  c. Body temperature
  d. Volume of water you drink in a day

Make the following measurements about your environment:
  e. Outdoor temperature
  f. Automobile speed limit on your street
  g. Distance to school
  h. Total mass of ingredients in your favorite cake or pie recipe
  i. Mass of your favorite sports equipment

Figure 2–14 *A triple-beam balance is one of the instruments used to measure mass in grams. Can mass in kilograms be measured by a triple-beam balance? Explain your answer.*

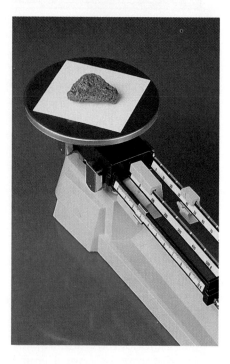

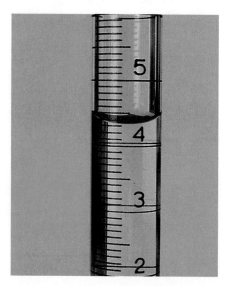

Figure 2–16 *A graduated cylinder is used to measure volume. To get an accurate measurement, where should you read the markings on the graduated cylinder?*

On the basis of its name, you probably guessed that a triple-beam balance has three beams. Each beam is marked in grams. The front beam is the 10-gram beam. Markings divide the front beam into 10 segments of 1 gram each. On some triple-beam balances, each 1-gram segment is further divided into units of one-tenth gram. The middle beam, often called the 500-gram beam, is divided into 5 segments of 100 grams each. The back beam, or 100-gram beam, is divided into 10 segments of 10 grams each. Based on this information, what is the largest mass you can measure on a triple-beam balance?

To measure the mass of a solid, such as a small pebble, you should follow these steps. First, place the pebble on the flat pan of the balance. Then slide the rider on the middle beam notch by notch until the pointer drops below zero. Move this rider back one notch. Next, slide the rider on the back beam notch by notch until the pointer drops below zero. Move this rider back one notch. Finally, move the rider on the front beam notch by notch until the pointer points exactly to the zero mark. The mass of the object is equal to the sum of the readings on the three beams.

If you want to find the mass of a powder or of crystals, you will have to place the sample on a sheet of filter paper on top of the pan. You must never place such a sample directly on the pan itself. The mass of the filter paper must first be determined. Once this is done, you can pour the sample onto the filter paper and find the mass of the filter paper and sample combined. Finally, by subtracting the mass of the filter paper from the combined mass of the filter paper and sample, you will get the mass of the sample.

You can use a similar method to find the mass of a liquid. As you might imagine, you must never pour a liquid directly onto the pan of the triple-beam balance. Instead, first place an empty beaker or flask on the pan and find its mass. Then pour the liquid into the container and find the combined mass of the liquid and the container. Now it is a simple process to subtract the mass of the container from the combined mass of the container and liquid. This will give you the mass of the liquid.

Measuring Volume

As you know, the liter is the basic unit of volume in the metric system. However, most of the measurements you will make in science will be in milliliters or cubic centimeters. Recall that 1 milliliter equals 1 cubic centimeter.

To find the volume of a liquid, scientists use a graduated cylinder. See Figure 2–16. A graduated cylinder is marked off in 1-milliliter segments. Each line on a graduated cylinder is 1 milliliter. To measure the volume of a liquid, pour the liquid into a graduated cylinder. You will notice that the top surface of the liquid is curved. To determine the volume of the liquid, read the milliliter marking at the bottom of the curve. (This curve is called the meniscus.) Suppose a liquid has a volume of 10 mL. How many cubic centimeters is this?

To find the volume of a solid that is rectangular in shape, you will use a metric ruler. A rectangular solid is often called a regular solid. The volume of a regular solid is determined by multiplying the length of the solid times the width times the height. The formula you can use to find the volume of a regular solid is:

Volume = length times width times height

or

$$\mathbf{v = l \times w \times h}$$

As you might expect, most of the solids you will measure will not be regular solids. Such solids are called irregular solids. Because the solid has an irregular shape, you cannot measure its length, width, or height. Are you stuck? Not really.

To determine the volume of an irregular solid, you will go back to the graduated cylinder. First fill the cylinder about half full with water. Record the volume of the water. Then carefully place the solid in the water. Record the volume of the solid and water combined. Subtract the volume of the water from the combined volume of the water and solid. The result will be the volume of the irregular solid. What units should you use for your answer?

ACTIVITY THINKING

How Good Is Your Guess?

Guess the metric measurements of each of the following items. Be sure to use the correct units.

a. Temperature of your classroom

b. Length of a paper clip

c. Mass of a penny

d. Distance from your classroom to the cafeteria

e. Volume of a paper cup

f. Volume of a shoebox

Now use the appropriate scientific tools to measure each item.

How good were your guesses?

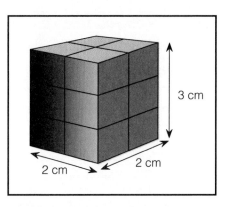

Figure 2–17 *What is the volume of this rectangular block in cubic centimeters?*

Figure 2–18 *A Celsius thermometer is used to measure temperatures such as those experienced by a polar bear in Alaska. What is the temperature of the ice-water mixture in the beaker?*

Measuring Temperature

You already know that temperature is measured with a thermometer. In the laboratory you will use a Celsius thermometer for temperature measurements. Each segment on a Celsius thermometer is equal to 1 degree Celsius. Many Celsius thermometers go as low as −25° so that temperatures below the freezing point of water (0°) can be measured.

Within the glass tube of a Celsius thermometer is a colored liquid. The liquid is usually mercury or alcohol. In order to measure the temperature of a substance, place the thermometer in the substance. The liquid in the thermometer will begin to change level (go up or go down). Wait until the liquid stops changing level. Then read the number next to the mark on the thermometer that lines up with the top of the liquid. This number is the temperature of the substance.

ACTIVITY

CALCULATING

Metric Conversions

Use conversion factors to make the following metric conversions. *Do not write in this book.*

10 m =	_____	km
2 km =	_____	cm
250 mL =	_____	L
2000 g =	_____	kg
10 kg =	_____	mg
1500 cc =	_____	L

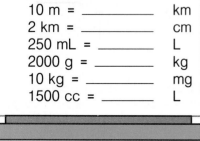

2–2 Section Review

1. Identify the instruments used to measure length, mass, volume, and temperature.
2. Each side of a regular solid is 5 centimeters long. What is the volume of the solid?

Critical Thinking—*Relating Concepts*

3. If you want to find the density of an irregular object, what tools will you need? How will you go about making this measurement?

Elbows to Fingertips

Have you complained to your teacher yet that you do not like the metric system? If so, perhaps you should read about some ancient systems of measurement. You might just decide that the metric system makes a lot of sense.

The Egyptians: The Egyptians are credited with having developed the most widespread system of measuring length in the ancient world. Developed around 3000 BC, the Egyptian standard of measurement was the *cubit.* The cubit was based on the length from the elbow to the fingertips. The cubit was further divided into *digits* (the length of a finger), *palms,* and *hands.* As you can see, body parts were the basis for most measurements.

The cubit may not seem like a very accurate measurement as the length of an arm varies from person to person. To avoid any confusion, a standard cubit made of granite was developed. All cubit sticks used in Egypt were measured against the standard granite cubit. And while this may not seem all that precise, the Egyptians built the great pyramids with incredible accuracy using the cubit!

The Greeks and Romans: Around 1000 BC, the Greeks developed a new system of measuring length. The basic unit of measurement was called the *finger* (again, body parts were popular). Sixteen fingers equaled a *foot* in the Greek system. Over time the influence of the Greeks diminished and the Romans became the dominant culture in the ancient world. The Romans adjusted the Greek system and divided the Greek foot into twelve *inches.* (Although the lengths have changed, we still use feet and inches in the United States.) The Romans then decided that five foots equaled a *pace.* And finally, one thousand paces equaled what they called a *mile.*

So the next time you are asked to measure something in meters or centimeters, remember—it could be worse. You could have to measure the distance from one place to another by placing your arm down over and over again.

Laboratory Investigation

Uncertainty of Measurements

Problem

How accurately can matter be measured?

Materials *(per station)*

Station 1:	meterstick
Station 2:	metric ruler
	regular object
Station 3:	graduated cylinder
	beaker with colored liquid
Station 4:	triple-beam balance
	small pebble
Station 5:	graduated cylinder
	beaker of water
	irregular object
Station 6:	Celsius thermometer
	beaker with ice and water
	paper towel

Procedure 🔺

1. Station 1: Use the meterstick to measure the length and width of the desk or lab table. If the table is irregular, measure the shortest width and the longest length. Express your measurements in centimeters.

2. Station 2: Use the metric ruler to find the volume of the regular object. Express the volume in cubic centimeters.

3. Station 3: Use the graduated cylinder to find the volume of the colored liquid in the beaker. Then pour the liquid back into the beaker. Express your measurement in milliliters.

4. Station 4: Place the pebble on the pan of the triple-beam balance. Move the riders until the pointer is at zero. Record the mass of the pebble in grams. Remove the pebble and return all riders back to zero.

5. Station 5: Fill the graduated cylinder half full with water. Find the volume of the irregular object. Express the volume of the object in cubic centimeters. Carefully remove the object from the graduated cylinder. Pour all of the water back into the beaker.

6. Station 6: Use the Celsius thermometer to find the temperature of the ice water. Record the temperature in degrees Celsius. Remove the thermometer and carefully dry it with a paper towel.

Observations

Your teacher will construct a large class data table for each of the work stations. Record the data from each work station in the class data table.

Analysis and Conclusions

1. Do all the class measurements have the exact same value for each station?

2. Which station had measurements that were most nearly alike? Explain why these measurements were so similar.

3. Which station had measurements that were most varied? Explain why these measurements were so varied.

4. **On Your Own** Calculate the average (mean) for the class data for each work station.

Study Guide

Summarizing Key Concepts

2-1 The Metric System

▲ The standard system of measurement used by all scientists is the metric system.

▲ The basic unit of length in the metric system is the meter. One meter is equal to 100 centimeters or 1000 millimeters.

▲ One kilometer is equal to 1000 meters.

▲ The basic unit of mass in the metric system is the kilogram. One kilogram is equal to 1000 grams.

▲ Weight is a measure of the force of attraction due to gravity. The basic unit of weight in the metric system is the newton.

▲ Although mass is a constant, weight can change depending on location.

▲ The basic unit of volume in the metric system is the liter. One liter contains 1000 milliliters or 1000 cubic centimeters.

▲ One cubic centimeter is equal in volume to 1 milliliter.

▲ Density is defined as the mass per unit volume of an object.

▲ The basic unit of temperature in the metric system is the degree Celsius.

▲ Dimensional analysis is a method of converting from one unit to another by multiplying the given quantity by a conversion factor whose value is one.

2-2 Measurement Tools

▲ A metric ruler is used to measure length. It is divided into centimeters and millimeters.

▲ A triple-beam balance is used to measure mass.

▲ A graduated cylinder is used to find the volume of a liquid or the volume of an irregular solid.

▲ The volume of a regular solid can be determined by multiplying its length by its width by its height.

▲ A Celsius thermometer is used to measure temperature.

Reviewing Key Terms

Define each term in a complete sentence.

2-1 The Metric System

metric system	kilogram
meter	gram
centimeter	milligram
millimeter	weight
kilometer	newton
light-year	density
liter	Celsius
milliliter	dimensional analysis
cubic centimeter	conversion factor

Chapter Review

Content Review

Multiple Choice

Choose the letter of the answer that best completes each statement.

1. The basic unit of length in the metric system is the
   a. kilometer.
   b. meter.
   c. liter.
   d. light-year.
2. A cubic centimeter is equal in volume to a
   a. kilogram.
   b. graduated cylinder.
   c. milliliter.
   d. millimeter.
3. The amount of matter in an object is called its
   a. density.   c. mass.
   b. volume.   d. weight.
4. Pure water freezes at
   a. 100°C.   c. 0°C.
   b. 32°C.   d. 10°C.
5. A graduated cylinder is divided into
   a. grams.
   b. degrees Celsius.
   c. milliliters.
   d. grams per milliliter.
6. To measure the mass of a solid, you should use a
   a. graduated cylinder.
   b. triple-beam balance.
   c. meterstick.
   d. bathroom scale.
7. Each side of a cube is 4 cm. Its volume is
   a. 16 cc.   c. 16 mL.
   b. 128 cc.   d. 64 cc.
8. In dimensional analysis, the conversion factor must be equal to
   a. the numerator.   c. 1.
   b. the denominator. d. 10.

True or False

If the statement is true, write "true." If it is false, change the underlined word or words to make the statement true.

1. The prefix *kilo-* means <u>one-thousandth</u>.
2. The <u>liter</u> is the basic unit of volume in the metric system.
3. The force of attraction between objects is called <u>gravity</u>.
4. Your <u>weight</u> on the moon would be the same as it is on the Earth.
5. Degrees Celsius are used to measure <u>volume</u>.
6. Density is <u>volume</u> per unit <u>mass</u>.
7. The boiling point of water is <u>100°C</u>.
8. The amount of space an object takes up is called its <u>mass</u>.

Concept Mapping

Complete the following concept map for Section 2–1. Refer to pages A6–A7 to construct a concept map for the entire chapter.

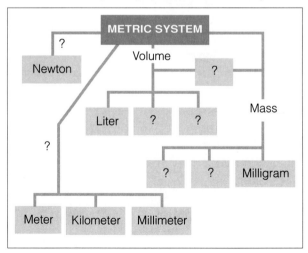

Concept Mastery

Discuss each of the following in a brief paragraph.

1. Describe the importance of a standard system of measurement.
2. Explain why mass is constant whereas weight can change.
3. Discuss the different metric units of length and explain when you might use each one.
4. Describe density in terms of mass and volume. Why is density such an important quantity?
5. Your friend wants you to convert kilograms to meters. Explain why that is not possible.
6. The Earth is about 5 billion years old. Yet some of the light that reaches Earth from distant stars began its journey before the Earth was formed. What does that tell you about the distance to those stars? Explain your answer.

Critical Thinking and Problem Solving

Use the skills you have developed in this chapter to answer each of the following.

1. **Applying concepts** What tool or tools would you use to make the following measurements? What units would you use to express your answers?
   a. Volume of a glass of water
   b. Length of a sheet of paper
   c. Mass of a liter of milk
   d. Length of a soccer field
   e. Volume of an irregular object
   f. Mass of a hockey puck
   g. Ocean temperature
2. **Making calculations** Use dimensional analysis to convert each of the following.
   a. A blue whale is about 33 meters in length. How many centimeters is this?
   b. The Statue of Liberty is about 45 meters tall. How tall is the statue in millimeters?
   c. Mount Everest is about 8.8 kilometers high. How high is it in meters?
   d. A Ping-Pong ball has a mass of about 2.5 grams. What is its mass in milligrams?
   e. An elephant is about 6300 kilograms in mass. What is its mass in grams?
3. **Relating concepts** Explain why every substance has a characteristic density, but no substance has a characteristic mass.

4. **Designing an experiment** A prospector is trying to sell you the deed to a gold mine. She gives you a sample from the mine and tells you it is pure gold. Design an experiment to determine if the sample is pure gold or "fools" gold. *Hint:* You will want to use the concept of density in your experiment.

5. **Using the writing process** Although the metric system is used throughout the world, it has not been officially adopted by the United States. Write a letter to the editor of your local newspaper in which you explain why the United States should or should not convert to the metric system.

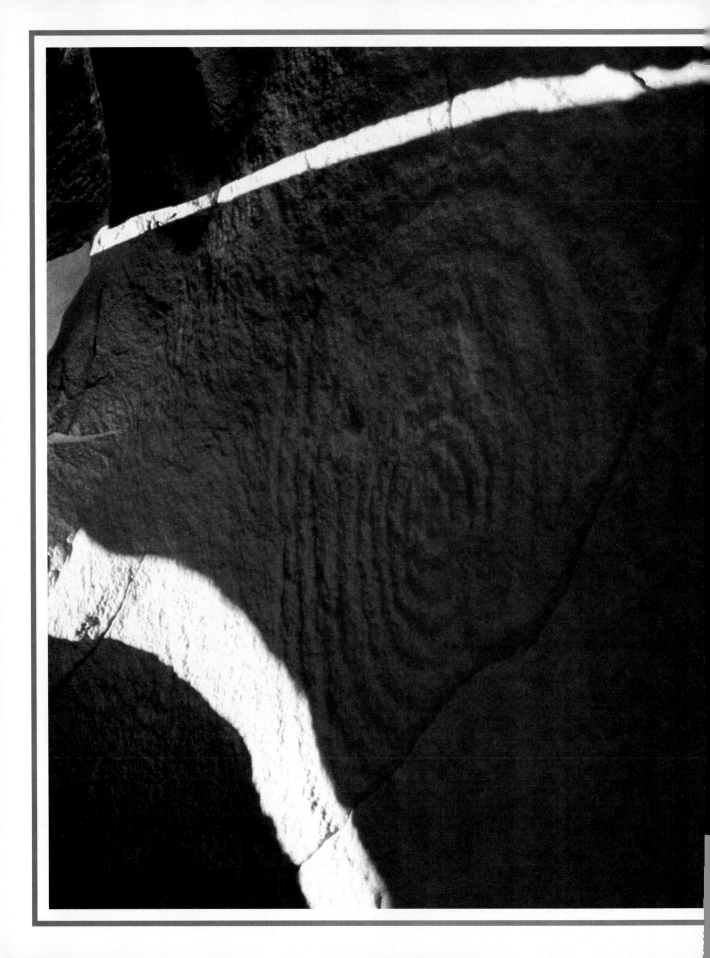

Tools and the Sciences

Guide for Reading

After you read the following sections, you will be able to

3–1 Exploring the Microscopic World

- Compare compound light microscopes and electron microscopes.

3–2 Exploring the Universe

- Compare refracting and reflecting telescopes.
- Relate the different types of telescopes to the electromagnetic spectrum.

3–3 Exploring the Earth

- Describe the tools used to study the Earth's oceans, crust, and atmosphere.

In the desert of northwestern New Mexico lies an interesting riddle. Two mysterious spirals are carved on a cliff wall behind three slanting stones. At noon on the first day of summer, a single ray of sunlight passes between two of the stones and strikes the larger of the two spirals through its center. At noon on the first day of spring and the first day of autumn, two rays of sunlight pass between the three stones and strike both spirals. At noon on the first day of winter, two rays of sunlight pass between the three stones and strike the large spiral on both sides. What do these spirals mean—and who carved them?

The mysterious spirals and slanting rocks are believed to be part of an astronomical observatory—a place where events in the sky were studied. Scientists think that the people who built the observatory were Anasazi Indians, who lived in the area long before Columbus discovered America.

Modern astronomers have built far more complex observatories. But although the tools of today are more advanced, the basic ways in which scientists try to solve the mysteries of nature may not be very different from those used by the Anasazi Indians. In this chapter you will learn about some of the tools used to explore the world.

Journal *Activity*

You and Your World What would it be like to live in the Southwest before the time of Columbus? Imagine you are a member of the Anasazi Indian tribe. In your journal, describe a typical day in your life.

First winter sunlight at the Anasazi observatory.

Dutchman's Dilemma

If you enjoyed the story of Anton van Leeuwenhoek, you may find the humorous poem *The Microscope* by Maxine Kumin a pleasant reading adventure.

Figure 3–1 *Some of the inhabitants of the microscopic world include bacteria (right) and protists (left).*

3–1 Exploring the Microscopic World

In 1676, a letter was sent to the Royal Society in London (the leading scientific group of that time) that would change forever the way we look at our world. The letter was sent by Anton van Leeuwenhoek, a Dutch drapery-maker who was also an amateur scientist. In his letter, van Leeuwenhoek described his observations of a drop of water. What made his observations so astounding was his announcement that he had seen ''living creatures in rain water.'' Van Leeuwenhoek called these creatures ''animalcules.''

What van Leeuwenhoek had seen were microscopic organisms, or organisms too small to be seen with the eye alone. Van Leeuwenhoek opened the door to that hidden world by using a simple microscope. Today, over three hundred years later, modern microscopes that van Leeuwenhoek could not even have dreamed would exist have been built. And our exploration of the microscopic world has come well beyond ''animalcules.'' But one thing remains the same: The door to the microscopic world is still open and there is still much to be discovered. Perhaps one day it will be a letter from you that astounds the scientific world. Remember, van Leeuwenhoek was not a professional scientist, just an

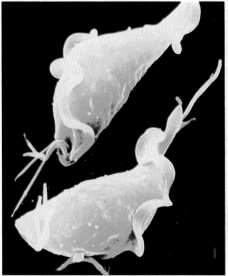

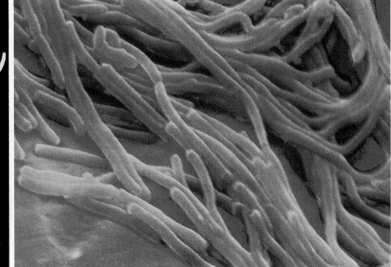

ordinary person with curiosity. Sound like anyone you know?

Microscopes have played an important role in scientific research ever since van Leeuwenhoek's discovery in 1676. **Microscopes are instruments that produce larger-than-life (magnified) images, pictures, or even videotapes.** Most microscopes use light rays to produce a magnified image of an object. Such microscopes are called optical microscopes (optical refers to light).

Optical Microscopes

Have you ever looked at an insect or other object under a magnifying glass? If so, then you have used a type of microscope known as a simple microscope. A magnifying glass is a simple microscope because it has only one **lens.** A lens is a curved piece of glass. As light rays pass through the glass, they bend. In some kinds of lenses, this bending of light rays increases the size of an object's image.

Scientific lenses are usually made of glass. However, any clear, transparent curved object can act as a lens. Take a look at a leaf that has dew or raindrops on it. If you look carefully through a drop, you will notice that the portion of the leaf under the drop is magnified. Why? The top of a drop of water is curved, much like a lens. Can you think of other examples of lenses that occur naturally? *Hint:* You are using two of them right now.

Figure 3–2 *Notice how these drops of water act as lenses, magnifying parts of the leaf.*

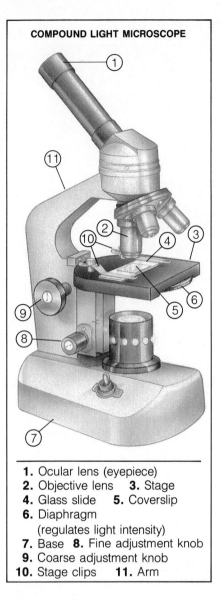

COMPOUND LIGHT MICROSCOPE

1. Ocular lens (eyepiece)
2. Objective lens   **3.** Stage
4. Glass slide   **5.** Coverslip
6. Diaphragm
   (regulates light intensity)
7. Base   **8.** Fine adjustment knob
9. Coarse adjustment knob
10. Stage clips   **11.** Arm

Figure 3–3 *This diagram is of a typical compound light microscope. What is another word for the eyepiece?*

Activity Bank

Life in a Drop of Water, p.108

The microscope that you will become most familiar with in your science courses is the **compound light microscope.** A compound light microscope has more than one lens. Like a magnifying glass, a compound microscope uses light to make objects appear larger. A magnifying glass can produce an image a few times larger than the actual object. But by using two lenses, a compound microscope can produce an image up to 1000 times the size of the actual object.

To use a compound microscope, the object to be viewed is first placed between a transparent glass slide and a thin coverslip. Then the slide with coverslip is mounted on the stage of the microscope. See Figure 3–3. Light, usually from a small light bulb at the base of the microscope, passes through the object and then through both lenses. The lens at the bottom of the microscope tube, or the lens closest to the object being observed, is called the objective lens. The lens at the top of the microscope tube, which is the lens through which you look, is called the eyepiece lens, or ocular lens. The magnification of the microscope is equal to the product (multiplication) of both lenses. For example, if the objective lens has a magnification power of 40 and the eyepiece lens has a magnification power of 10, then the object you observe will be magnified 400 times (40 times 10).

Appendix D at the back of this textbook provides detailed instructions on the use of a compound light microscope. Review this appendix carefully before you use a microscope.

Compound light microscopes are extremely useful to life scientists because they allow for the observation of living microscopic organisms. That is, an organism does not have to be killed to be viewed under a compound light microscope. Other microscopes do not have this advantage.

When compound light microscopes were first developed, people assumed that magnification power could be increased by making better and better lenses. It turns out that even the best compound microscopes can magnify no more than about 1000 times. After that, the image begins to get fuzzy and lose detail. Are there ways to magnify objects more than 1000 times? The answer is yes, but such magnification does not involve the use of light.

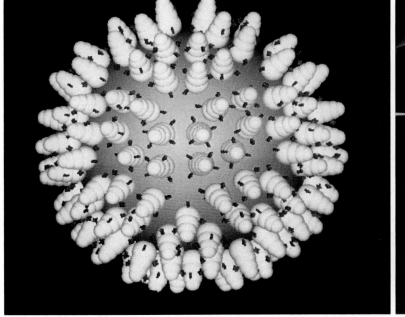

Electron Microscopes

Light microscopes are certainly very useful. But because of the limitation on their magnification power, they cannot be used to observe extremely small objects: living things such as viruses or individual atoms and molecules that make up matter. These objects have been revealed, however. So the question is how?

Today a great deal of scientific research is done using the **electron microscope.** An electron microscope uses a beam of tiny particles called electrons instead of light rays. (Electrons are among the particles that make up an atom.) The beam of electrons is not focused through a lens, as light rays in a light microscope are, but rather by magnets. Objects viewed with an electron microscope can be magnified up to 1 million times. Using electron microscopes, scientists can observe the smallest organisms as well as individual atoms and molecules. In most cases, the magnified image of an object is viewed on a television screen.

There are several types of electron microscopes. You will now read about two of the most common.

TRANSMISSION ELECTRON MICROSCOPE   One type of electron microscope is called the transmission electron microscope (TEM). In a TEM, electrons are

Figure 3–4 *Keep in mind that microscopes are but one tool scientists use. Modern science and technology now includes the use of lasers in eye surgery (right) and computer-generated images of disease-causing viruses (left).*

Figure 3–5 *Using a TEM, scientists can study the internal structure of organisms like this single-celled diatom.*

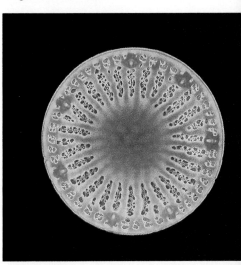

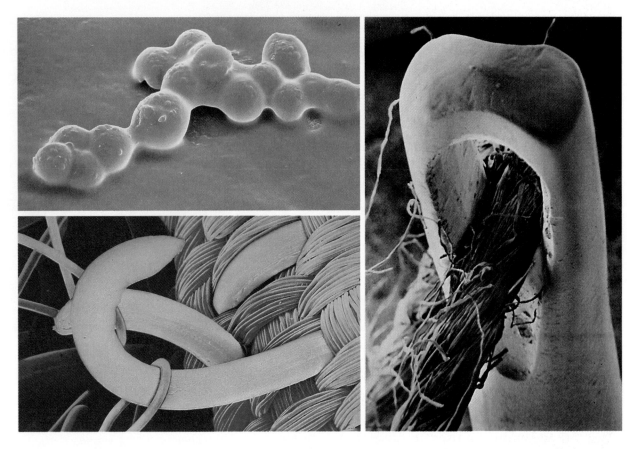

Figure 3–6 *Photographs taken through an SEM can provide amazing 3-D images. Here you see tiny scent globules used on scratch-and-sniff stickers (top left), a Velcro™ hook (bottom left), and a thread passing through a needle (right).*

beamed at an object in much the same way light rays are in a compound light microscope. The magnified image of the object is then observed on a television screen. A photograph of the image can also be produced. TEMs are useful to scientists when observing the inside of an object, such as the structures found in a cell.

SCANNING ELECTRON MICROSCOPE   Another type of electron microscope is called the scanning electron microscope (SEM). In an SEM, electrons are beamed at an object and reflected (bounced back) from the object. The reflected electrons produce a three-dimensional photograph of the object. SEMs are useful for observing the outer structure of an object, such as the arrangement of atoms in a solid.

Both TEMs and SEMs do present one problem. The object to be viewed must be sliced into very thin layers and placed in a vacuum (a space from which all air has been removed). As you might expect, such a procedure means that the object cannot be alive. So TEMs and SEMs cannot be used to view living things.

Figure 3-7 *Notice the unmagnified pollen grains visible on the flower (top). Then look at pollen grains that have been magnified 60 times (center). This three-dimensional image of pollen grains (bottom) has been magnified 378 times. What kind of microscope took the photograph at the bottom?*

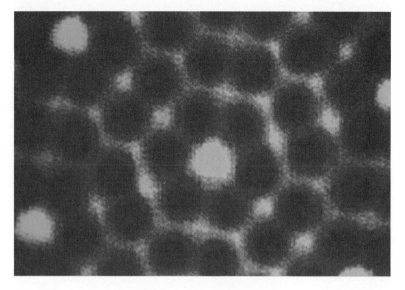

Looking Through Barriers

So far we have been discussing the use of microscopes to produce magnified images of an object. Sometimes, however, scientists do not need to magnify an object but rather to look inside the object. Today there are several tools available that allow scientists to "look through barriers."

X-RAYS Do you know someone who has had a broken bone? Perhaps you have had one yourself. A doctor could cut you open to examine the break, but that would not be a very pleasant experience. As you probably know, there is a better way to do it.

For almost one hundred years, scientists have been using a type of radiation known as X-rays to see through objects. X-rays are similar to light rays, but they are invisible to the eye. Unlike light, however, X-rays pass easily through soft objects such as skin and muscle. But X-rays are blocked by dense objects such as bone. As a result, X-rays can be used to take pictures of bones inside an organism.

CT SCANS Computed Tomography, or CT scan, is a new technique that produces cross-sectional pictures of an object. An X-ray machine in a CT-scanner is used to take up to 720 different exposures of an object. Each picture shows a "slice" of the object. A computer analyzes and combines the exposures to construct a picture. Among its many uses, a CT scan can provide detailed pictures of body parts such as the human brain.

Figure 3–9 *MRI images help scientists study the inside of the body. What important organ can be studied from this MRI?*

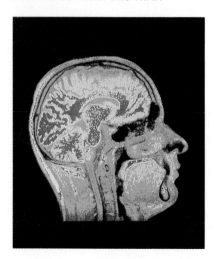

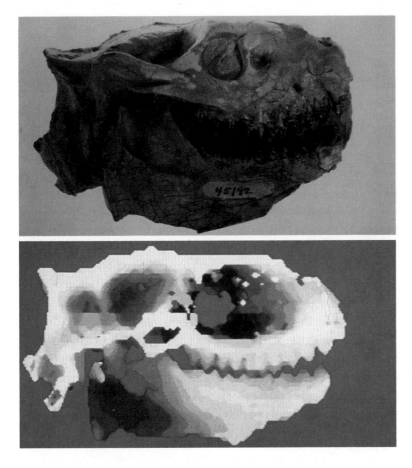

Figure 3-10 *Because this 30-million-year-old skull of a small mammal (top) was a rare find, scientists did not want to break it open. By using a CT scanner, scientists were able to get a three-dimensional view of the inside of the skull (bottom).*

MRI Magnetic resonance imaging, or MRI, is another tool that helps scientists see inside objects. MRI uses magnetism and radio waves to produce images. Scientists can use MRI to study the structure of body cells without harming the living tissue.

3-1 Section Review

1. What is a microscope?
2. Explain the basic difference between a compound light microscope and an electron microscope.
3. Of the three types of microscopes discussed, what kind of research can be performed only by using a compound light microscope?

Connection—*Science and Technology*

4. It has been said that many great discoveries await the tools needed to make them. What does this statement mean to you?

Guide for Reading

Focus on these questions as you read.

▶ What is a telescope?

▶ How do different types of telescopes provide different views of the universe?

3–2 Exploring the Universe

As you just learned, the invention of the microscope opened up a previously unknown world. It was not quite the same case with the world beyond planet Earth. People's understanding that the Earth is part of a vast universe did not require any special tools. Even the earliest known records indicate that people wondered about the twinkling lights they observed in the night sky. But knowledge of the universe was quite limited. It was not until the invention of the telescope that people truly began to explore the universe. The moons of Jupiter and the rings of Saturn, for example, did not become visible until the telescope was invented.

The telescope is an instrument used to view and magnify distant objects in space. **Scientists use a variety of telescopes to study the Universe: optical telescopes, radio telescopes, infrared telescopes, ultraviolet telescopes, and X-ray telescopes.** You will now read about these different types of telescopes and discover what kinds of information they provide.

Figure 3–11 *The invention of the telescope opened the door to the incredible vastness of outer space and showed that our sun is but the tiniest drop in an ocean of stars.*

Optical Telescopes

The first telescopes used by early astronomers were optical telescopes.(Remember that the term optical refers to light.) An optical telescope collects and focuses visible light from distant objects such as stars and galaxies. Using a series of mirrors, lenses, or a combination of the two, the telescope magnifies the image formed by the light. The two types of optical telescopes are refracting telescopes and reflecting telescopes.

REFRACTING TELESCOPES In a **refracting telescope,** a series of lenses is used to focus light. (You should recall that an optical microscope uses a series of lenses to magnify microscopic objects.) In general, the larger the lens, the greater the light-gathering power of a telescope. The size of a telescope is given as the diameter of its largest lens. The world's largest refracting telescope is the "40-inch" telescope at Yerkes Observatory in Wisconsin. This telescope has a light-gathering power about 40,000 times greater than the human eye!

REFLECTING TELESCOPES In a **reflecting telescope,** a series of mirrors is used to collect and focus light from distant objects. For technical reasons, the mirrors in a reflecting telescope can be built much larger than the lenses in a refracting telescope. One of the world's largest reflecting telescopes is the "200-inch" Hale telescope at Mount Palomar in California. Telescopes like the Hale telescope can observe objects billions of light-years from Earth. They literally open the door to the very edge of the universe.

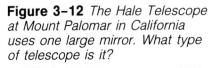

Figure 3–12 *The Hale Telescope at Mount Palomar in California uses one large mirror. What type of telescope is it?*

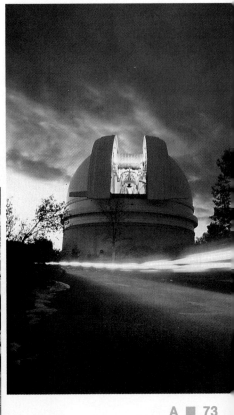

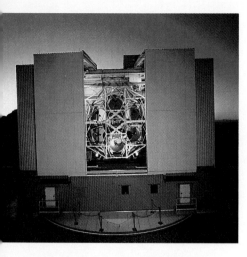

Figure 3-13 *The Multiple Mirror Telescope atop Mount Hopkins in Arizona uses six mirrors.*

MULTIPLE MIRROR TELESCOPES   Large reflecting telescopes are extremely difficult and expensive to build. The mirrors in such telescopes must be perfectly constructed and flawless. For many years scientists believed that a 5-meter mirror (approximately 200 inches) was about the largest mirror they could construct. To get around that problem, the Multiple Mirror Telescope was constructed. Sitting high atop Mount Hopkins in Arizona, the Multiple Mirror Telescope contains six ''72-inch'' mirrors. The six mirrors work together to collect light from distant stars and provide even greater power than the single large mirror in the Hale telescope.

NEW ADVANCES IN OPTICAL TELESCOPES   Many new types of optical telescopes are being designed and tested throughout the world. How many will go from the drawing board to actual construction remains to be seen. Each of these new types of telescopes uses a different design to enlarge the size of the mirror it houses. One of the most recently developed telescopes is the Keck telescope in Mauna Kea, Hawaii. The Keck telescope has a "400-inch" mirror. How have scientists solved the problem of building such a large mirror? In a sense, they haven't. For the Keck telescope actually contains 36 individual mirror segments joined together in what looks like a beehive. The 36 mirror segments make the Keck telescope the most powerful optical telescope on Earth—at least until an even newer and larger telescope is built.

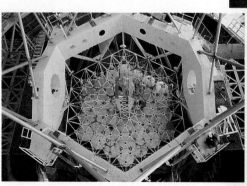

Figure 3-14 *The Keck telescope in Hawaii houses a "400-inch" mirror made up of 36 segments (inset).*

Radio Telescopes

No doubt when you think of stars you think of visible light. After all, that's what you see when you look up at the night sky. Visible light, however, is only one part of the **electromagnetic spectrum.** In addition to visible light, the electromagnetic spectrum includes forms of "light" we cannot detect with our eyes. These forms of invisible light include X-rays, ultraviolet rays and infrared rays, and radio waves. And as it turns out, many stars give off both visible and invisible light. Is there a way to view distant stars using invisible light? Yes, but obviously not with an optical telescope.

In Chapter 1, you learned about the discovery of radio astronomy by Karl Jansky and Grote Reber. At that time we said that radio telescopes opened up a new view of the universe—and oh what a view! Because many stars give off mainly radio waves (not visible light), the invention of the radio telescope provided scientists with an opportunity to study the universe in a new and exciting way. It was almost as if a huge part of the universe had been hidden from us, waiting for the discovery of the radio telescope to reveal itself.

An optical telescope can be thought of as a bucket for collecting light waves from space. A **radio telescope** can be thought of as a bucket for collecting radio waves from space. In most radio telescopes, a curved metal dish gathers and focuses radio waves onto an antenna. The signal picked up

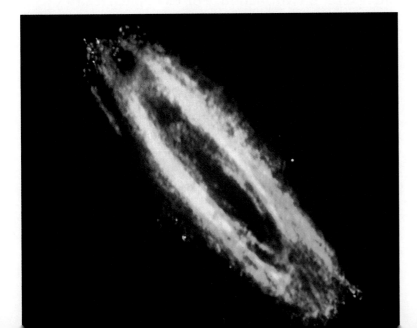

Figure 3–15 Radio telescopes have produced this image of the Andromeda galaxy, one of our nearest neighbors in space.

Figure 3–16 *The Very Large Array in New Mexico is made up of 27 radio telescopes.*

by the antenna is fed into computers, which then produce an image of the object giving off the radio waves. Radio telescopes are usually mounted on movable supports so they can be directed toward any point in the sky. These telescopes have been able to collect radio waves from objects as far away as 14 billion light-years!

In the desert of New Mexico stands a group of 27 radio telescopes known as the Very Large Array, or VLA. The VLA is extremely useful because it combines the radio-wave detecting power of 27 individual radio telescopes. With the VLA, scientists can get a clearer picture of many objects in space than they can with a single radio telescope.

Infrared and Ultraviolet Telescopes

In general, stars are the only objects in space that give off visible light. And some stars are so dim they do not give off enough visible light to be easily observed. But all objects, even dark, cold objects such as planets, give off infrared rays. Recall that infrared is part of the electromagnetic spectrum. Another term for infrared is heat energy. Unfortunately, infrared rays from distant objects in space are not easily detected once they enter Earth's atmosphere. So telescopes that operate using infrared rays are carried out of the atmosphere.

In January, 1983, the Infrared Astronomy Satellite, or *IRAS,* was launched. *IRAS,* the first **infrared telescope** in space, soon provided scientists with new and exciting information. For example, *IRAS* detected heat waves from newborn stars in clouds of gas and dust 155,000 light-years from Earth. *IRAS* also collected information that suggests that the distant star Vega is surrounded by a giant cloud of matter. This cloud may be an early stage in the development of planets. If so, *IRAS* has given us the first view of planets beyond our solar system.

Like infrared, ultraviolet light is an invisible form of light in the electromagnetic spectrum. In order to detect ultraviolet light given off by objects, scientists have constructed **ultraviolet telescopes.** Ultraviolet rays from space do not pass easily through Earth's atmosphere. So ultraviolet telescopes, like infrared telescopes, are usually carried out of the Earth's

ACTIVITY

WRITING

A New Comet

One of the first achievements of IRAS was finding a new comet in our solar system. Using library and other reference sources, find out the name of that comet—and the mystery of its triple name. Report your findings in a brief essay.

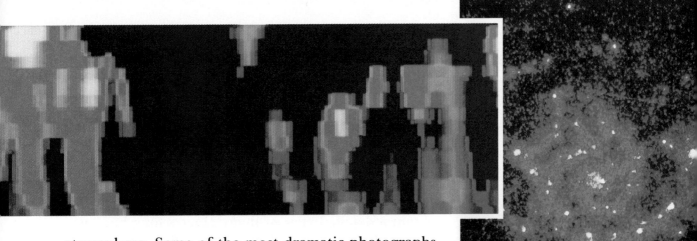

atmosphere. Some of the most dramatic photographs taken with ultraviolet telescopes are of our own sun, which gives off huge amounts of ultraviolet light daily. One of the primary tasks of the *Hubble Space Telescope,* which you will read about shortly, is to detect ultraviolet rays from space using an on-board ultraviolet telescope.

X-ray Telescopes

X-rays are another form of electromagnetic radiation given off by stars. In fact, almost all stars give off X-rays. By now you should not be surprised to learn that **X-ray telescopes** have been constructed to detect the invisible X-rays from space. Of all the forms of light in the electromagnetic spectrum, X-rays are the least able to pass through Earth's atmosphere. (A good thing because if they did, no life as we know it could survive on Earth.) So X-rays from space can only be detected by X-ray telescopes sent into orbit above the Earth.

In 1970, the first X-ray telescope, called *Uhuru,* was launched. *Uhuru* gave scientists their first clear view of X-ray sources in the sky. *Uhuru* and other orbiting X-ray telescopes have provided a wealth of information about the life cycle of stars, particularly what happens to very massive stars as they begin to age and die.

Space Telescope

In Chapter 2, you learned about a flaw in the 2.4-meter mirror of the *Hubble Space Telescope.* What you did not learn at that time was that the *Hubble Space Telescope* also houses several other kinds of

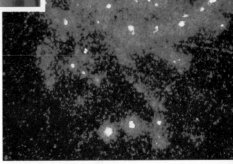

Figure 3–17 *Compare the infrared image of the Dorados nebula (left) with the ultraviolet image of a spiral galaxy (right).*

Figure 3–18 *This X-ray image shows the remains of a star that exploded in what is called a supernova.*

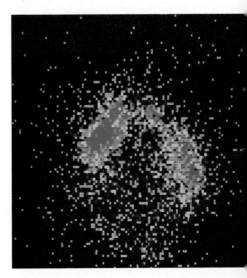

Figure 3–19 *Here you see the* Hubble Space Telescope *floating in orbit above the Earth, as photographed from the Space Shuttle.*

telescopes. So you can think of the *Hubble Space Telescope* as a combination of telescopes—each of which provides a different picture of the universe. In fact, one of the first important discoveries of the *Hubble Space Telescope* was made by its ultraviolet telescope. In 1991, the ultraviolet telescope revealed what could be the beginning of a new solar system forming around a star called Beta Pictoris.

Scientists have nicknamed the *Hubble Space Telescope* the "eye in the sky." With it, they can obtain a detailed view of many objects long hidden from earthbound telescopes. Although the primary mirror is not working perfectly, it still enables the *Hubble Space Telescope* to provide excellent photographs of many distant objects. Combined with the other telescopes on board, the *Hubble Space Telescope* promises to expand our knowledge of the universe in as dramatic a fashion as van Leeuwenhoek's microscope opened up the microscopic world.

3–2 Section Review

1. Compare refracting and reflecting telescopes.
2. Name and describe three types of telescopes that detect invisible light.

Connection—*You and Your World*
3. Doctors use X-rays to take pictures of broken bones and other body parts. Why can the doctor's X-rays pass through the atmosphere but X-rays from space cannot?

Guide for Reading

Focus on this question as you read.

▶ *What tools are used by scientists to study the Earth's oceans, crust, and atmosphere?*

3–3 Exploring the Earth

We have learned about a few of the tools scientists use to study the microscopic world and the world of outer space. Now you will spend some time learning about the ways in which scientists explore the planet Earth. **In simple terms, we can think of the Earth as being divided into three main parts— water, land, and air.**

Exploring Earth's Oceans

More than 70 percent of the Earth is covered by water, and most of that water is found in the oceans. It's no wonder, then, that Earth is often referred to as the water planet.

Scientists use research vessels called submersibles to explore the oceans. Some submersibles carry only scientific instruments; others carry people as well. One kind of submersible is called a **bathysphere** (BATH-ih-sfeer). A bathysphere is a small, sphere-shaped diving vessel. It is lowered into the water from a ship by a steel cable. Because it remains attached to the ship, the bathysphere has limited movement.

A **bathyscaph** (BATH-ih-skaf) is a more useful submersible. It is a self-propelled submarine observatory that can move about in the ocean. Bathyscaphs have reached depths of more than 10,000 meters while exploring some of the deepest parts of the ocean.

The bathyscaph *Alvin* has made thousands of dives into the ocean depths. Some of *Alvin's* discoveries have helped scientists learn more about life on the ocean floor. During one dive, scientists aboard

Figure 3–20 *Among the many unusual organisms discovered by the submersible* Alvin *was a new form of life called tube worms.*

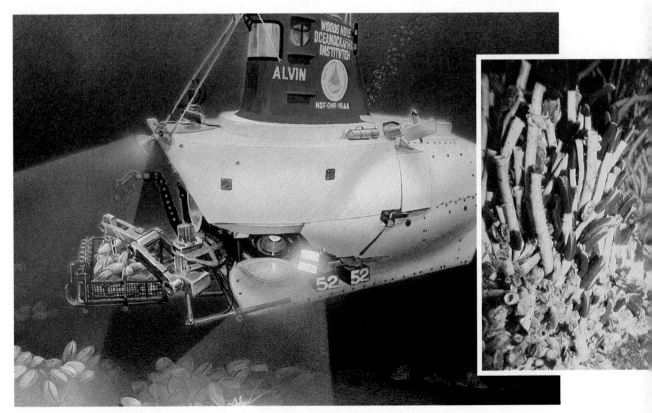

ACTIVITY

READING

Dangerous Depths

Do you love an action-packed adventure story? If so, you will want to read *Twenty Thousand Leagues Under the Sea,* by Jules Verne.

Alvin found several communities of unusual ocean life near vents, or natural chimneys, in the ocean floor. The vents discharge poisonous hydrogen sulfide into the water. Water temperatures near the vents reach 350°C. The combination of high temperatures and deadly hydrogen sulfide should make the existence of life forms near the vents impossible. But as the scientists discovered, giant tube worms, clams, mussels, and other strange life forms make their homes near the vents. These life forms exist without any sunlight. Some scientists suggest that conditions near the vents may be similar to conditions on distant planets. So the discoveries made by *Alvin* may help astronomers study the possibility of life on other worlds.

In September 1985, another submersible made a remarkable discovery. This submersible is a robot craft that can be guided along the ocean floor from a ship on the surface. The robot craft discovered the remains of the famous steamship *Titanic.* The ship was lying on the ocean floor in very deep water off the coast of Newfoundland, Canada. In 1912, on its maiden voyage, the *Titanic* struck an iceberg and quickly sank.

Figure 3–21 *Notice the robot craft as it is about to explore the wreck of the* Titanic.

Exploring Earth's Crust

We often tend to take the land we walk on for granted. "Solid as the Earth," is a common phrase. And most of the time, it makes sense. But in the 1980s, residents of Mexico, Armenia, and California (to name just a few places) felt the Earth move beneath their feet. What they felt, in case you haven't guessed, was an earthquake.

Detecting and measuring the strength of earthquakes is an important task for scientists who explore the Earth's crust. One day their studies may enable them to predict earthquakes so that people in the affected area can be warned before the earthquake strikes. Today, unfortunately, our ability to predict earthquakes is limited. But we are well able to detect and measure them using a tool called the **seismograph** (SIGHZ-muh-grahf).

A seismograph is a fairly simple instrument. It consists of a weight attached to a spring or wire. Because the weight is not attached directly to the Earth, it will remain nearly still even when the Earth moves. A pen is attached to the weight. Beside the pen is a rotating drum wrapped with paper.

Figure 3–22 *This collapsed California highway is evidence of the tremendous energy unleashed during an earthquake.*

ACTIVITY

CALCULATING

Earthquake Waves

Earthquake waves, or seismic waves, travel at a speed 24 times the speed of sound. The speed of sound is 1250 km/hr. How fast do seismic waves travel?

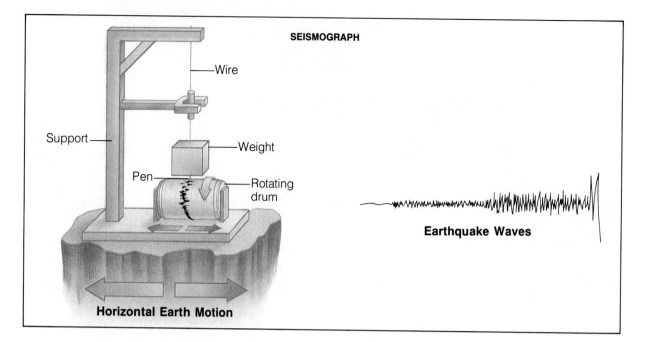

Wire

Support

Weight

Pen

Rotating drum

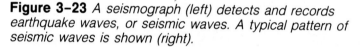

Earthquake Waves

Horizontal Earth Motion

Figure 3–23 *A seismograph (left) detects and records earthquake waves, or seismic waves. A typical pattern of seismic waves is shown (right).*

Because the pen is attached to the weight, it also remains nearly still when the Earth moves. But not so for the drum, which is attached to the Earth and moves with the Earth. When the Earth is still, the pen records an almost straight line on the rotating drum. However, when an earthquake occurs, the pen records a wavy line as the drum moves with the Earth. What kind of line would be recorded during a violent earthquake?

Scientists can determine the strength of an earthquake by studying the height of the wavy lines recorded on the drum. The higher the wavy lines, the stronger the earthquake. Using the seismograph, scientists can detect an earthquake at almost the instant it occurs—anywhere on Earth!

Exploring Earth's Atmosphere

Scientists use many tools to study the Earth's atmosphere. Weather balloons and satellites transmit data to weather tracking stations around the world, enabling scientists to predict the weather far better than they could in the past. Wind vanes measure the speed and direction of the wind, an important thing to know if you are trying to determine if a nearby

Figure 3–24 *Among the most modern scientific tools are weather satellites which, among other things, can be used to track potentially dangerous hurricanes.*

storm is coming your way. Other instruments measure the humidity (amount of moisture in the atmosphere) and air temperature. The list of instruments to study the atmosphere goes on and on. In this section, we will learn about one instrument you may already be familiar with—the **barometer.**

A barometer is a device that measures air pressure. Although you probably don't often think about it, air is a form of matter and therefore has mass. And as you learned in Chapter 1, the Earth's gravity pulls matter toward the Earth. In simple terms, air pressure is a measure of the force of the atmosphere pushing down on every point on the Earth due to gravity.

There are two different types of barometers. One type is a mercury barometer. A mercury barometer consists of a glass tube closed at one end and filled with mercury (a silvery liquid). The open end of the glass tube is placed in a container of mercury. At sea level, air pushing down on the mercury in the container supports the column of mercury in the glass tube at a certain height. As the air pressure decreases, the column of mercury drops. What will happen if the air pressure increases?

Figure 3–25 *When air pressure increases, the column of mercury rises in the barometer tube (right). What happens when air pressure decreases (left)?*

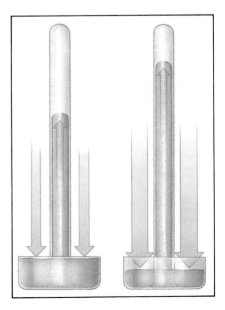

Figure 3–26 *An aneroid barometer (inset) is used to measure air pressure anywhere from your hometown to the foggy banks off Kruzof Island in Alaska.*

A more common type of barometer is called an aneroid (AN-er-oid) barometer. See Figure 3–26. An aneroid barometer consists of an airtight metal box from which most of the air has been removed. A change in air pressure causes a needle to move and indicate the new air pressure. Perhaps you have an aneroid barometer at home or in your school. If so, see if you can discover for yourself the relationship between rising and falling air pressure and the weather in your area.

ACTIVITY

CALCULATING

A Water Barometer

Mercury has a density of 13.5 g/cm³. Water has a density of 1.0 g/cm³. If standard air pressure supports a column of mercury 76 cm high, how high would a column of water be supported at this pressure?

3–3 Section Review

1. What are some of the tools used to explore the Earth's oceans, crust, and atmosphere?
2. Can a seismograph be used to predict earthquakes? Explain your answer.

Critical Thinking—*Applying Concepts*

3. Using the term density, explain why air pressure is related to altitude (distance above sea level).

CONNECTIONS

Modern Medicine— Ancient Cure

While preparing bone specimens for microscopic study, a young college student in Detroit made a fascinating discovery. She found that shining ultraviolet light on the bones made them glow yellow-green. The yellow-green color was characteristic of a *modern medicine* called tetracycline used to combat disease. But the bone specimen was over 1600 years old and was part of a skeleton found in the Nubian desert in Africa. How could ancient bones contain a modern medicine?

The answer to the puzzling question lies with a bacterium called streptomyces, which produces tetracycline naturally. Streptomyces also makes up about 60 percent of the bacteria living in Nubian soil. Scientists believe that the streptomyces flourished at the bottom of mud bins used to store grain.

Normally, tetracycline leaves a bitter taste in food. So it is unlikely the people of that time ate the contaminated grain at the bottom of the bin—if they could avoid it. However, every few years that region suffered through serious famines and food became very scarce. At such times we would normally expect disease to rise as people's strength was sapped by the lack of food. But it was during such famines that people were willing to eat the contaminated grain. After all, bitter food is better than no food at all. The ancient people in the Nubian desert could not know how fortunate they were. For just when they needed it most, they ate the grain with the life-saving medicine—without ever realizing how a bacterium was protecting them from disease!

Laboratory Investigation

Constructing a Telescope

Problem

How does a refracting telescope work?

Materials *(per group)*

meterstick
2 lens holders
2 convex lenses or magnifying glasses of different sizes
unlined index card (to be used as a screen)
card holder

Procedure 🔬

1. Put the two lenses in the lens holders and place them on the meterstick. Put the index card in its holder and place it between the two lenses.

2. Aim one end of the meterstick at a window or an electric light about 3 to 10 meters away. Light given off or reflected by an object will pass through the lens and form an image of the object on the screen (index card). Carefully slide the lens nearer to the light source back and forth until a clear, sharp image of the light source forms on the screen.

3. The distance between the center of the lens and the sharp image is called the focal length of the lens. Measure this distance to obtain the focal length of that lens. Record your measurement.

4. Turn the other end of the meterstick toward the light source. Without disturbing the screen or the first lens, determine the focal length of the second lens.

5. Point the end of the meterstick that has the lens with the longer focal length toward a distant object. Without changing the positions of the lenses, take the

screen out of its holder and look at the distant object through both lenses. You may have to adjust the lenses slightly to focus the image. You have now constructed a refracting telescope.

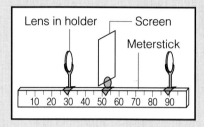

Observations

1. What was the focal length of the first lens? The second lens?

2. How does the image seen through the lens with the shorter focal length differ from the image seen through the lens with the longer focal length?

3. How does the image of an object seen through the lens with the longer focal length appear different from the object itself?

Analysis and Conclusions

1. In a telescope, the lens with the shorter focal length is called the eyepiece. The lens with the longer focal length is called the objective. You can calculate the magnifying power of your telescope by using the following formula:

$$\text{Magnifying power} = \frac{\text{Focal length of objective}}{\text{Focal length of eyepiece}}$$

Using the formula, calculate the magnifying power of your telescope.

2. **On Your Own** What is the relationship between the telescope's magnifying power and the ratio between the focal lengths of the lenses?

Study Guide

Summarizing Key Concepts

3-1 Exploring the Microscopic World

▲ A microscope is an instrument that produces larger-than-life images of an object.

▲ A magnifying glass is a simple optical microscope with a single lens.

▲ Compound light microscopes contain an eyepiece lens and an objective lens. The magnifying power of the microscope is determined by multiplying the magnifying powers of the lenses.

▲ In order to magnify an object greater than 1000 times, an electron microscope is used. Electron microscopes use a beam of electrons, rather than light, to magnify an object.

▲ The two main types of electron microscopes are the transmission electron microscope (TEM) and the scanning electron microscope (SEM).

▲ X-rays, CT scans, and MRI scans are some of the tools scientists use to look "inside" an object.

3-2 Exploring the Universe

▲ A telescope is an instrument used to view and magnify distant objects.

▲ The two types of optical telescopes are the refracting telescope, which uses a series of lenses, and the reflecting telescope, which uses a series of mirrors to magnify an object.

▲ The electromagnetic spectrum includes visible light as well as infrared, ultraviolet, X-rays, and radio waves.

▲ Many objects in space give off radio waves, which can be observed through the use of a radio telescope.

▲ Infrared, ultraviolet, and X-ray telescopes each provide a different view of the universe.

3-3 Exploring the Earth

▲ In general terms, the Earth can be divided into water, land, and atmosphere.

▲ Scientists use submersibles such as the bathysphere and the bathyscaph to explore ocean depths.

▲ The seismograph is an instrument that detects and measures earthquakes.

▲ One of the most important tools used to study the atmosphere is the barometer, which measures air pressure.

Reviewing Key Terms

Define each term in a complete sentence.

3-1 Exploring the Microscopic World
lens
compound light microscope
electron microscope

infrared telescope
ultraviolet telescope
X-ray telescope

3-2 Exploring the Universe
refracting telescope
reflecting telescope
electromagnetic spectrum
radio telescope

3-3 Exploring the Earth
bathysphere
bathyscaph
seismograph
barometer

Chapter Review

Content Review

Multiple Choice

Choose the letter of the answer that best completes each statement.

1. A telescope that uses a series of mirrors to collect and magnify light from distant objects is called a
   a. compound light telescope.
   b. refracting telescope.
   c. reflecting telescope.
   d. none of these

2. A magnifying glass uses
   a. two lenses.   c. a single lens.
   b. a single mirror. d. two mirrors.

3. The highest magnifying power of a compound light microscope is
   a. 100.   c. 10,000.
   b. 1000.   d. 100,000.

4. To observe the outer structure of a virus, you would use a(an)
   a. TEM.
   b. compound light microscope.
   c. SEM.
   d. MRI.

5. Which telescope would be best placed in outer space?
   a. X-ray telescope
   b. infrared telescope
   c. ultraviolet telescope
   d. all of these

6. Optical telescopes detect
   a. X-rays.   c. infrared energy.
   b. visible light. d. radio waves.

7. The strength of an earthquake is measured by a(an)
   a. seismograph. c. MRI.
   b. bathyscaph.   d. series of lenses.

8. A barometer measures
   a. weather conditions.
   b. temperature.
   c. air pressure.
   d. precipitation.

True or False

If the statement is true, write "true." If it is false, change the underlined word or words to make the statement true.

1. In a compound light microscope, the lens closest to the object being observed is called the <u>objective lens</u>.
2. The magnifying power of a microscope is found by <u>dividing</u> the power of the objective lens by the power of the eyepiece lens.
3. One type of <u>compound light microscope</u> is the TEM.
4. The <u>magnetoelectric</u> spectrum includes both visible and invisible light.
5. A submersible that is attached directly to a ship on the ocean's surface is called a <u>bathyscaph</u>.

Concept Mapping

Complete the following concept map for Section 3–1. Refer to pages A6–A7 to construct a concept map for the entire chapter.

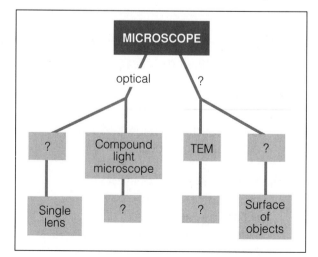

Concept Mastery

Discuss each of the following in a brief paragraph.

1. Discuss the uses and limitations of a compound light microscope, an SEM, and a TEM.
2. Van Leeuwenhoek's experiments with a drop of water have been compared to suddenly discovering that an entire family has been living in your house without your knowledge. Explain the meaning of this comparison.
3. How has our understanding of objects in space been limited by the tools we can use?
4. Explain the meaning of the statement, "There is more to light than meets the eye."
5. Describe the relationship between air pressure and density.

Critical Thinking and Problem Solving

Use the skills you have developed in this chapter to answer each of the following.

1. **Making charts** Construct a chart that shows the different types of telescopes and the kinds of energy each type can detect.
2. **Expressing an opinion** A great deal of money is spent each year on space exploration. Many people feel that this money could be better spent improving conditions on Earth. Other people feel that knowledge gained from space exploration will ultimately bring great benefits to human society. Still others suggest that scientific knowledge is valuable for its own sake and should not be thought of in terms of dollars and cents. What is your opinion? Explain your answer.
3. **Designing an experiment** Ocean water, unlike fresh water, contains salt. The amount of salt in ocean water is called salinity. Design an experiment to determine if the salinity of ocean water changes as the depth of the ocean changes.
4. **Drawing conclusions** At the beginning of this chapter we stated that the way the Anasazi Indians tried to solve the mysteries of nature may not be very different from those used by modern scientists. Now that you have completed the chapter, explain whether you agree or disagree with that statement.
5. **Using the writing process** If telescopes could talk, what stories would they tell? Write a telescope story. *Hint:* First decide what type of telescope you are.
6. **Using the writing process** You have been given the opportunity to travel back to the age of dinosaurs. Which of the tools discussed in this chapter would be most useful in your travels? Explain your answer.

SCIENCE GAZETTE

STEPHEN HAWKING: Changing Our View of the Universe

Scientists have long struggled to find the connection between two branches of physics. One of these branches deals with the forces that rule the world of atoms and subatomic particles. The other branch deals with gravity and its role in the universe of stars and galaxies. Physicist Stephen Hawking has set himself the task of discovering the connection. Leading theoretical physicists agree that if anyone can discover a unifying principle, it will certainly be this extraordinary scientist.

Dr. Hawking's goal, as he describes it, is simple. "It is complete understanding of the universe, why it is as it is and why it exists at all." In order to achieve such an understanding, Dr. Hawking seeks to "quantize gravity." Quantizing gravity means combining the laws of gravity and the laws of quantum mechanics into a single universal law.

▲ Stephen Hawking is a Lucasian professor of mathematics at Cambridge University—a position once held by Isaac Newton. Hawking has received numerous prizes for his work.

Dr. Hawking and other theoretical physicists believe that with such a law, the behavior of all matter in the universe, and the origin of the universe as well, could be explained.

Dr. Hawking's search for a unifying theory has led him to study one of science's greatest mysteries: black holes. A black hole is an incredibly dense region in space whose gravitational pull attracts all nearby objects, virtually "swallowing them up." A black hole is formed when a star uses up most of the nuclear fuel that has kept it burning. During most of its life as an ordinary star, its nuclear explosions exert enough outward force to balance the powerful inward force of gravity. But when the star's fuel is used up, the outward force ceases to exist. Gravity takes over and the star collapses into a tiny core of extremely dense material, possibly no bigger than the period at the end of this sentence.

Hawking has already proved that a black hole can emit a stream of electrons. Prior to this discovery, scientists believed that noth-

ing, not even light, could escape from a black hole. So scientists have hailed Hawking's discovery as "one of the most beautiful in the history of physics."

Probing the mysteries of the universe is no ordinary feat. And Stephen Hawking is no ordinary man. Respected as one of the most brilliant physicists in the world, Hawking is considered one of the most remarkable. For Dr. Hawking suffers from a serious disease of the nervous system that has confined him to a wheelchair, and he is barely able to move or speak. Although Dr. Hawking gives numerous presentations and publishes countless articles and papers, his addresses must be translated and his essays written down by other hands.

Hawking became ill during his first years at Cambridge University in England. The disease progressed quickly and left the young scholar quite despondent. He even considered giving up his research, as he thought he would not live long enough to receive his Ph.D. But in 1965, Hawking's life changed. He married Jane Wilde, a fellow student and language scholar. Suddenly life took on new meaning. "That was the turning point," he says. "It made me determined to live, and it was about that time that I began making professional progress." Hawking's health and spirits improved. His studies continued and reached new heights of brilliance. Today, Dr. Hawking is a professor of mathematics at Cambridge University who leads a full and active life.

Dr. Hawking believes that his illness has benefited his work. It has given him more time to think about physics. So although his body is failing him, his mind is free to soar. Considered to be one of the most brilliant physicists of all times, Dr. Hawking has taken some of the small steps that lead science to discovery and understanding. With time to ponder the questions of the universe, it is quite likely that Stephen Hawking will be successful in uniting the world of the tiniest particles with the world of stars and galaxies.

Are We Destroying the Greatest Creatures of the Sea?

During the late 1860s, a Norwegian inventor, Svend Foyn, invented a harpoon with a tip that exploded when it hit its target: a whale. This new weapon enabled whalers to kill their prey much faster and easier than ever before. Foyn's harpoon led to the development of modern whaling and the slaughter of the world's whales.

Since the beginning of this century, more than three million whales have been killed. Several species are now endangered. The number of blue whales, the largest living creatures, has dropped from 100,000 to less than 1,000. There are only small numbers of right whales and bowheads left. Many other species also are declining in number.

Most countries that once carried on commercial whaling, including the United States, have long since stopped. But a few, such as Japan and Norway, continue to hunt whales for profit. Whaling nations contend that they do not hunt endangered species, only those species that are still common. Conservationists argue that even whales of common species are dropping too rapidly in number. These people believe that, for several years at least, no whales of any species should be hunted.

STOPPING THE SLAUGHTER

In response to conservationists, the International Whaling Commission voted in 1982 to ban commercial whaling starting in 1986. Set up to regulate whaling, the commission has members from more than two dozen nations, the United States and whaling countries among them. But the ban does not guarantee that the killing will stop. For one thing, a country can withdraw from the commission at any time and kill all the whales it wants to.

Moreover, within 90 days after the ban was voted upon, Norway, Japan, and other whaling nations filed protests against it with the commission. Under commission rules, this exempts them from the ban.

Even so, however, the nations that protested may choose not to take advantage of their exemption. If they did take advantage of their exemption, their actions could

◄ One job of The International Whaling Commission is to control the killing of whales, such as these sperm whales.

prompt a strong re-
action from the
United States, which led
the campaign for the ban. Both
private businesses in the United
States and the federal government have been
urged by conservationists to boycott products from countries that continue to kill
whales. In fact, our government can even
place fishing restrictions on nations that
break whaling commission rules. These
restrictions would apply only in United States
waters. Our government can also bar fish
imports from nations that ignore the
commission.

Japan fishes heavily in United States waters. Norway and Japan sell millions of dollars of fish products to the United States
each year. If they do not go along with the
whaling ban, they could lose a great deal.

There is a chance, however, that the whaling countries could take a position on the
ban that the United States might find hard
to criticize. The commission allows certain
groups of people, such as Alaskan Eskimos,
to hunt a limited number of whales for their
own use. The Eskimos, the commission
reasons, need whale oil and
meat to live.

Japan and Norway contend that
many whalers in their countries need
to hunt whales commercially to live. Whaling is a tradition for these people just as it
is for the Eskimos. Why not, ask the Japanese and Norwegians, give their whalers the
same consideration as the Eskimos and let
them kill and sell a limited number of whales?

To do so, says environmentalist Allan
Thornton, in a report for the conservation
group Defenders of Wildlife, would "be a
disaster for whale conservation." He warns
it would be impossible to police the limits
on small-scale commercial whaling. Even
hunting by Eskimos, he adds, is endanger-
ing some whales. All whaling, not just commercial whaling, needs a second look,
according to Thornton.

AN AGE THAT HAS PASSED

Whaling was once a worldwide business, and brave men in sailing vessels roamed the globe to hunt the huge creatures. Oil from whales was burned in lamps. Whalebone was used in making women's undergarments. The teeth of some whales were used to make piano keys. Today, however, many whale products can be or have been replaced by other materials. But whale meat still has a market, most notably in Japan. So whaling can still be profitable, even if not as profitable as in the past.

Even in Japan, however, whale meat accounts for less than 1 percent of the protein eaten by the Japanese. Echoing conservationists, United States Representative Don Bonker noted in Congress, "There is no reason to continue commercial whaling at any level."

Conservationists view whales as a symbol. If people cannot preserve the largest animals on Earth, they say, there is little hope for any other part of nature.

Whales, moreover, play an important part in keeping the ocean environment balanced.

The largest whales, such as the blue whale, feed on tiny shrimplike creatures and other small organisms, collectively known as krill. The whales obtain the krill by straining it from the water with huge sievelike structures in their mouths called baleen, or whalebone.

The baleen whales are at the top of an important food chain. They eat krill, which feed on microscopic plants, which in turn convert the sun's energy and sea salts into food. The waste excreted by whales provides nutrients for microscopic plants and other organisms in the water. All in all, the relationship between the whale and the other organisms in the food chain is a neatly balanced natural cycle that constantly renews the food resources of the sea.

If the baleen whales disappear, the cycle will be broken. What will happen then? Scientists are not sure. But there is no doubt that the fragile balance of nature in the ocean would tip—and not in our favor.

WANTED!

Space Pioneers

Kansas City Star: January 12, 2021

WANTED:

Moon Miners and Engineers to provide new space colony with building materials. We're looking for people who can turn moon rocks and lunar topsoil into usable metals such as aluminum, magnesium, and titanium. These metals will be used to make tools and to build support structures for the colony. We also want workers who can extract silicon from the moon's silicates. Silicon is needed to make solar cells and computer chips. Glass that will be used for windows in space colony homes also comes from lunar silicates. And iron and carbon mined from the moon need to be turned into steel.

In addition, we're looking for lunar gold miners to search the moon's surface for deposits of gold, as well as nickel and platinum. And oxygen, which will be used for both life-support systems and rocket fuel, needs to be extracted from moon rocks.

erry had answered the advertisement. Now, in the year 2024, she was hard at work at Moon Mine Alpha.

Terry expertly plunged the heavy shovel of her bulldozer into the soil to pick up another load of valuable material. When she raised the shovel, it was filled with moon rocks and lunar dust. Terry dumped her cargo into her lunar hauler. "My last truckload of the day," she thought, jumping down from the bulldozer. "Now I can go watch the mass driver in action."

Terry swung into the driver's seat of the lunar hauler. Soon she was bumping along the moon highway, a dusty path her hauler and others like it had carved out of the lunar topsoil over the past few months.

◀ **A typical lunar colony with all the comforts of home!**

inner surface of the sphere. Here 10,000 people or more will live and work inside an earthlike environment powered by the sun. The Space Colony will be constructed of materials mined almost entirely on the moon.

RESOURCES IN SPACE

As many scientists see it, our growing needs for raw materials, energy, and jumping-off places for journeys to the planets and stars make us look into space. Where else is there a free, continuous supply of solar energy, uninterrupted by darkness or weather? Where else does weightlessness, which will aid in the construction of huge structures, exist? Where else is there an untapped source of minerals?

A wealth of energy and materials is available in space. Let's start with the moon, a mere 356,000 kilometers away. This natural satellite could be an important source of aluminum, iron, silicon, and oxygen. A permanent base established on the moon could supply all the resources needed to support space settlement and exploration. Although these resources are abundant on the Earth, bringing millions of tons of materials into space is out of the question!

The moon could become a gigantic "supply station" in the sky. Metals and lunar soil could be mined to build huge structures inside of which comfortable, earthlike homes would be constructed. Since the moon's grav-

Fifteen minutes later, she spotted the huge piece of machinery known as the mass driver. She saw the "flying buckets" of the mass driver suspended magnetically above special tracks. The buckets, filled with packages of lunar rocks, soon would be sent speeding along above these tracks by powerful magnetic forces. When the buckets reached high enough speed, they would fling their contents into space at 2.4 kilometers per second. At this speed, an object can escape the moon's gravity. Hundreds or thousands of kilometers away, a mass catcher would be waiting to grab the lunar cargo. The lunar materials would then be turned into fuel or building materials for a new space colony. Surely the mass driver, developed in the 1970s at the Massachusetts Institute of Technology, had proved to be a valuable tool for space colonization.

What will this space colony be like? Stationed nearly 400,000 kilometers from the Earth, a huge sphere more than 1.5 kilometers in diameter will rotate in space. The rotation will create artificial gravity on the

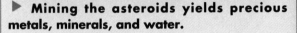

► **Mining the asteroids yields precious metals, minerals, and water.**

itational force is one sixth the strength of the Earth's, it would be cheaper and easier to build such space factories and colonies on the moon. These buildings could become part of the permanent moon base.

Almost half of the moon is made up of oxygen. This oxygen could be used to make rocket fuel. Liquid hydrogen mixed with liquid oxygen is a basic rocket fuel. Rockets bound for the outer planets could be launched more easily from the moon than from Earth, where the pull of gravity is six times greater.

A NEW FRONTIER

The moon is not the only source of natural materials in near space. Asteroids are also vast treasure houses of minerals. They contain metals such as nickel, iron, cobalt, magnesium, and aluminum. Phosphorus, carbon, and sulfur are also present on asteroids. And they may contain the precious metals gold, silver, and platinum. Asteroids are also important sources of water. One small asteroid can perhaps yield between 1 and 10 billion tons of water.

"Hey, Terry, how's it going?" The voice belonged to Bill, one of the workers who ran the mass driver.

"Oh, I still like being a moon miner," Terry answered, "but a few years from now, I hope to be mining the asteroids instead. It should be a challenge trying to capture a small asteroid or land on a big one."

"I hope you like traveling, Terry," Bill said with a worried look. "The trip could take months or years."

"It would be worth it," said Terry as she waved to Bill and headed to her two-room apartment under the plastic dome of Hadleyville. Turning on her TV set to watch live coverage from Earth of the 2024 Summer Olympics, Terry tuned in the *Moon Miner's Daily Herald*, a TV "newspaper." Suddenly, an advertisement caught her eye.

WANTED:
Asteroid Miners and Engineers to capture small asteroids and collect samples from larger asteroids. Workers must be willing to spend long periods of time far from home. Travel to the asteroid belt, which lies between the orbits of Mars and Jupiter about 160 to 300 million kilometers away, is required.

"Why not?" Terry thought as she began to type out a reply on her computer.

For Further Reading

> If you have been intrigued by the concepts examined in this textbook, you may also be interested in the ways fellow thinkers—novelists, poets, essayists, as well as scientists—have imaginatively explored the same ideas.

Chapter 1: What Is Science?

Adamson, Joy. *Born Free, a Lioness of Two Worlds.* New York: Pantheon.

Ames, Mildred. *Anna to the Infinite Power.* New York: Scribner.

Doyle, Sir Arthur Conan. *Adventures of Sherlock Holmes.* New York: Berkley Pub.

Freeman, Ira, and Mae Freeman. *Your Wonderful World of Science.* New York: Random House.

Chapter 2: Measurement and the Sciences

Clarke, Arthur C. *2001: A Space Odyssey.* New York: New American Library.

Duder, Tessa. *In Lane Three, Alex Archer.* Boston: Houghton-Mifflin.

Kohn, Bernice. *The Scientific Method.* Englewood Cliffs, NJ: Prentice-Hall.

Merrill, Jean. *The Toothpaste Millionaire.* Boston: Houghton-Mifflin.

Chapter 3: Tools and the Sciences

Asimov, Isaac. *Fantastic Voyage.* Boston: Houghton-Mifflin.

Merle, Robert. *The Day of the Dolphin.* New York: Simon & Schuster.

Walsh, Jill Paton. *Toolmaker.* New York: Seabury.

Activity Bank

Welcome to the Activity Bank! This is an exciting and enjoyable part of your science textbook. By using the Activity Bank you will have the chance to make a variety of interesting and different observations about science. The best thing about the Activity Bank is that you and your classmates will become the detectives, and as with any investigation you will have to sort through information to find the truth. There will be many twists and turns along the way, some surprises and disappointments too. So always remember to keep an open mind, ask lots of questions, and have fun learning about science.

OBSERVING A FISH

Many people keep fish in an aquarium. To be successful, you have to have a good idea of the kind of conditions a fish needs to survive. In this activity you will observe a fish in an environment you create. This is actually a long-term investigation because you will be responsible for caring for your fish after this activity is over. You and your classmates might want to keep records about the growth of your fish, the amounts and kinds of foods eaten, and any changes in your fish's behavior over time. In a later activity you will examine some of the water in your fish's aquarium under a microscope. Then you will use another tool of the scientist.

Materials

aquarium or large unbreakable clear plastic container

gravel

water plants

several rocks

small goldfish

fish food

hand lens

brown paper bag (slit along the sides)

plastic bucket

pitcher (1L)

Procedure

1. Wash the aquarium or jar thoroughly. Use table salt on a sponge to clean the glass. Do not use soap. Thoroughly rinse the aquarium or jar when you are finished. Place the aquarium or jar near a window where it will get some light for part of the day. **CAUTION:** *Do not try to move the aquarium or jar when it is filled with water.*

2. Place the gravel in a plastic bucket. Place the bucket in a sink. Let cold water run into the bucket. (You may also do this in the backyard if you have access to a garden hose.) Put your hand into the bucket and gently move the gravel around. The gravel dust will become suspended in the water and will be carried away as the water runs over the top of the bucket. You can stop rinsing the gravel when clear water runs out. Carefully empty the water out of the bucket.

3. Pour the gravel into the aquarium or jar. Smooth it out.

4. Place the sheet of brown paper over the gravel. Use a pitcher to gently pour water onto the paper in the aquarium or jar. Stop adding water when the aquarium or jar is two-thirds full. Remove the paper.

5. Position the rocks in the gravel. Place the plants in the gravel. Try to make your underwater scene look realistic. Now gently add water almost to the top edge of the aquarium or jar. Do not add fish to the aquarium or jar for a few days. (During this time the water may become cloudy. It will clear up over time.)

6. A salesperson in a pet store will place the fish you select in a plastic bag. Float the plastic bag in the aquarium or jar for 20 minutes to allow the temperature of the water in the bag and in the aquarium or jar to equalize. Open the bag and let your fish swim into its new home. Allow the fish a few minutes of quiet time to explore its new surroundings.

7. Now add a small pinch of food to the surface of the water.

8. Use the hand lens to observe the fish's head.

Observations

1. How did the fish behave in its new home?
2. What fins did the fish use to move itself forward in the water? What fins did it use to remain in the same place?
3. How did the fish behave when you placed a pinch of food in the tank?
4. Describe what you observed when you used the hand lens to examine the fish's head.
5. In what part of the aquarium or jar does the fish spend most of its time?

Analysis and Conclusions

1. In what ways is a fish able to live in water?
2. How does your fish get food?

Going Further

You might like to read more about keeping fish. Your library or pet shop will have a selection of books about how to keep and raise fish. Report to your class on what you learn.

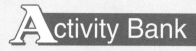

WHAT DO SEEDS NEED TO GROW?

If you completed the investigation on page A34, you are now familiar with some of the conditions molds need in order to grow. In this activity you will learn about conditions that must be present in order for plant seeds to grow. You may wish to do this investigation with several classmates. Each person can grow a different kind of seed, or each person can test a different variable. Share your information with one another and with the rest of the class when the activity is completed.

You Will Need

4 plastic flowerpots or 4 plastic food
   containers
tray or 4 saucers
potting soil
bean or radish seeds
2 thermometers
masking tape

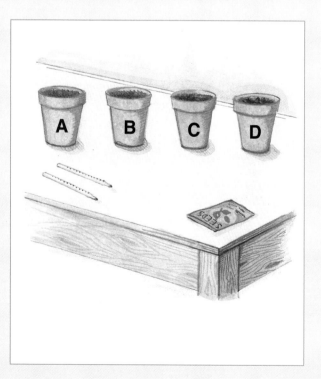

Procedure

1. If you use plastic food containers, make sure they are clean. Have an adult punch some holes in the bottom of the containers. The holes will let excess water drain out of the containers. Use the saucers or tray to collect any water that runs out of the pots when they are watered.

2. Fill the pots or containers almost to the top with potting soil.

3. Place several seeds in each pot. Gently press the seeds into the soil. You may wish to add a thin layer of soil on top of the seeds.

4. Use the masking tape to label the pots A through D.

5. Water pot A and place it on a windowsill. This is your control plant. Water this plant when the soil feels dry to the touch.

6. Water pot B and place it in a dark place. Make sure this pot also receives water when the top of the soil feels dry to the touch.

7. Tape a thermometer to the outside of pot C. Do not water pot C now or for the duration of the activity. Place it on a windowsill next to pot A. The thermometer will provide the temperature for all the pots placed on the windowsill.

8. Tape the other thermometer to pot D. Water pot D and place it in a refrigerator.

9. In a data table similar to the one shown on page 103, record the temperature of each pot as indicated by its attached thermometer. Continue to take the temperature of the pots each day for three weeks. Record these readings.

DATA TABLE

TEMPERATURE		
Day	Windowsill	Refrigerator
1		
2		
3		
4		
5		
6		
7		
8		
9		
10		
11		
12		
13		
14		
15		
16		
17		
18		
19		
20		
21		

Observations

1. What did you observe in each pot?
2. In which pots did the seeds grow best?
3. Which pots showed the poorest results?
4. Why is pot A considered a control?

Analysis and Conclusions

1. Why did you need a control?
2. What variable were you testing in pot B?
3. What variable were you testing in pot C?
4. What variable were you testing in pot D?
5. On the basis of your observations, what conditions do seeds need to begin to grow well?
6. It might be argued that there were two variables in pot D. What was the other variable? Was it a critical factor in the activity? Why or why not?

Activity Bank

Calculating the density of a regular solid such as a cube is easy. Measure the sides of the object with a metric ruler and calculate the volume. Place the object on a balance to determine its mass. Then use the formula D = M/V to calculate the object's density. But can you determine the density of an object that has an irregular shape and is not easy to measure? A rock, for example. It's easy when you know how. Follow along and you can become the density calculator for your class.

Materials

graduated cylinder
rock
small piece of metal pipe
large nut or bolt
triple-beam balance
metric ruler
string

Procedure and Observations

1. Select one of the objects whose density you wish to calculate. Place the object on a balance and determine its mass. Enter the mass in a data table similar to the one shown on page 105.

2. Place some water in the graduated cylinder. Look at the water in the cylinder from the side. The water's surface will be shaped like a saucer. Notice that the water level dips slightly in the center. Add water carefully until the lowest part of the water's surface (the bottom of the dip) is at one of the main division lines on the side of the graduated cylinder. Enter the water-level reading in your data table.

3. You are going to determine the volume of your irregularly shaped object by

water displacement. To do this, first tie a piece of string around the object you are going to use. Make sure the string is well tied.

4. Hold the end of the string and carefully lower the object into the water in the graduated cylinder. Read the new water level. Enter this reading in your data table. Subtract the first water-level reading from the second to determine the volume of the object. Enter this volume in your data table.

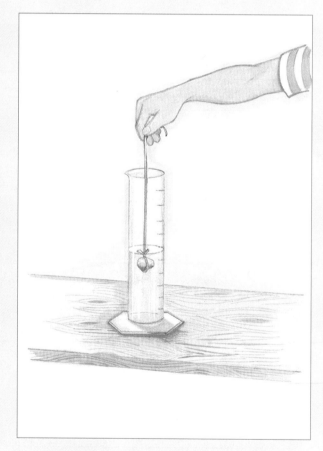

5. Repeat this procedure for each remaining object.

6. Use the formula D = M/V to calculate the density of each object you selected.

DATA TABLE

Object	Mass	First Water Level	Second Water Level	Water Displaced (mL)

Analysis and Conclusions

1. What is the volume of an object whose dimensions are 1.0 cm × 6.0 cm × 2.0 cm? Remember to include the proper units.

2. If the mass of this object is 60 g, what is its density?

3. What are the densities of the objects you measured?

4. Which object is made of the densest material?

Think About This

1. If an object with a density of 10 g/cm^3 is cut into two equal pieces, what is the density of each piece? Why?

2. Could the water displacement method be used to determine the volume of a rectangular object as well as an irregularly shaped object?

3. Why is the density of a substance important?

DAZZLING DISPLAYS OF DENSITIES

Throw a rock into a pond and it sinks beneath the surface of the water. Throw a rubber ball into a pond and it bobs along on the surface. Why do some things float in water while others sink? The answer has to do with density. An object floats only if it is less dense than the substance it is in. In this activity you will make your own investigation into density.

Materials

2 250-mL beakers
cooking oil (about 125 mL)
ice cube
salt
spoon or small sheet of tissue paper
(optional)
hard-boiled egg or small uncooked potato
medicine dropper
dishwasher liquid
food coloring

Procedure

1. Fill a beaker half-full with cooking oil. Very gently place an ice cube on the surface of the oil. What happens to the ice cube? Watch the ice cube for the next 15 to 20 minutes. What happens as the ice cube melts?

2. Use the dishwasher liquid to thoroughly clean the beaker. Fill the beaker half-full with water. Make sure you measure the amount of water you put into the beaker.

3. Add plenty of table salt to the water. Stop adding salt when the water becomes cloudy. The amount of salt you add will vary depending upon the amount of water you use.

4. Add the same amount of water you used in step 2 to another beaker. Do not add salt to the water in this beaker. Slowly and gently pour the unsalted water into the beaker that contains the water you added salt to. You may need to pour the water onto a spoon or piece of tissue paper so that it hits the salt water more gently.

5. Gently place the egg or small potato in the beaker. Describe and draw what you see.

6. Clean the two beakers. Add a small amount of hot tap water, about 10 mL, to one of the beakers. Add a few drops of food coloring to the hot water. Make sure you add enough food coloring so that the color can easily be seen.

7. Fill the other beaker with cold tap water.

Food coloring

8. Use the medicine dropper to pick up a few drops of the hot colored water.

9. Place the tip of the medicine dropper in the middle of the cold water in the other beaker. Slowly squeeze a drop of the hot colored water into the cold water. Describe and draw a picture of what you observe.

Analysis and Conclusions

1. Explain what you observed when you watched the ice cube in the oil in step 1.

2. Explain your observations regarding the egg in the beaker of water.

3. What does this investigation tell you about the density of hot water compared to the density of cold water?

4. Predict what will happen if you repeat steps 6 through 9, but this time add a drop or two of cold colored water to a beaker of hot water.

LIFE IN A DROP OF WATER

Just as good building tools can help a carpenter produce a fine home, so can good scientific tools aid a scientist in a variety of endeavors.

In this activity you will use one of the basic tools of life science: a microscope, a tool that lets scientists study worlds too small to be seen with the unaided eye.

You Will Use

microscope
glass slide
coverslip
water from your aquarium or pond water
medicine dropper

CAUTION: *Before you begin, make sure that you understand how to use a microscope.* Follow your teacher's instructions exactly. Examine the illustration of a microscope in Appendix D. A microscope is an expensive and valuable tool. Exercise care when using it and when using the slide and coverslip as well.

Now You Can Begin

1. Make sure that your microscope is in the correct position before you use it. Have your teacher check your setup before you begin. Use the illustration on page 115 in your textbook to familiarize yourself with the parts of your microscope.

2. There are several lenses on a microscope. The lens nearest the eye is called the ocular. The lenses closest to the slide are called the objectives. Note that each lens has a number etched on it. The number tells you how many times a particular lens magnifies the image that is viewed through it. Note the number on the ocular and the num-

ber on the smallest objective lens. Multiply one number by the other. This will tell the total magnification when these two lenses are used together. Enter the magnification near any drawing you make of what you observe.

3. Pick up a glass slide from your supply table. You will make a slide of a drop of water from your aquarium. (If you do not have an aquarium you can examine pond water that your teacher will supply. **CAUTION:** *Do not try to collect pond water without the help of an adult.*) Place one drop of aquarium water in the center of your slide.

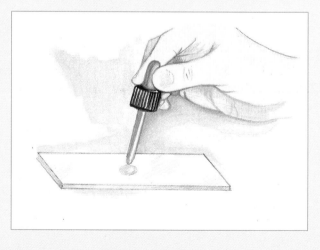

4. Pick up one of the coverslips and hold it as shown in the illustration. Carefully lower the coverslip onto the drop of water.

5. Place the slide on the microscope. Make sure the smallest, or low-power, lens is in position. Look through the ocular. Carefully turn the coarse adjustment knob until the image is in focus. Use the fine adjustment knob to get a clear image. Move the slide slowly back and forth. Draw what you observe.

6. Repeat the procedure with a drop of tap water.

7. When you are finished, follow your teacher's instructions for cleaning up.

Observations

1. What kinds of things did you observe in the drop of water from the aquarium?

2. Did these organisms move around or remain in one place?

3. What did you observe in the drop of tap water?

Analysis and Conclusions

1. How has the microscope helped scientists to study the natural world?

2. How can you explain the differences you observed in the aquarium water and the tap water?

Going Further

You can examine some other substances. Make a plan of study and check with your teacher before you proceed.

The metric system of measurement is used by scientists throughout the world. It is based on units of ten. Each unit is ten times larger or ten times smaller than the next unit. The most commonly used units of the metric system are given below. After you have finished reading about the metric system, try to put it to use. How tall are you in metrics? What is your mass? What is your normal body temperature in degrees Celsius?

Commonly Used Metric Units

Length   The distance from one point to another

meter (m)
　A meter is slightly longer than a yard.
　1 meter = 1000 millimeters (mm)
　1 meter = 100 centimeters (cm)
　1000 meters = 1 kilometer (km)

Volume   The amount of space an object takes up

liter (L)
　A liter is slightly more than a quart.
　1 liter = 1000 milliliters (mL)

Mass   The amount of matter in an object

gram (g)
　A gram has a mass equal to about one paper clip.

　1000 grams = 1 kilogram (kg)

Temperature   The measure of hotness or coldness

degrees
Celsius (°C)
　0°C = freezing point of water
　100°C = boiling point of water

Metric–English Equivalents

2.54 centimeters (cm) = 1 inch (in.)
1 meter (m) = 39.37 inches (in.)
1 kilometer (km) = 0.62 miles (mi)
1 liter (L) = 1.06 quarts (qt)
250 milliliters (mL) = 1 cup (c)
1 kilogram (kg) = 2.2 pounds (lb)
28.3 grams (g) = 1 ounce (oz)
°C = 5/9 × (°F – 32)

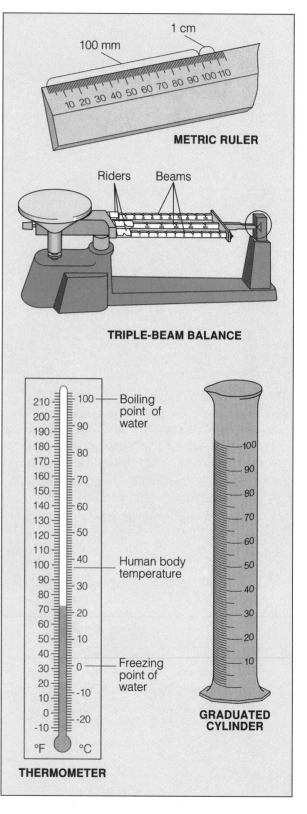

METRIC RULER

TRIPLE-BEAM BALANCE

THERMOMETER

GRADUATED CYLINDER

Appendix B

Glassware Safety

1. Whenever you see this symbol, you will know that you are working with glassware that can easily be broken. Take particular care to handle such glassware safely. And never use broken or chipped glassware.
2. Never heat glassware that is not thoroughly dry. Never pick up any glassware unless you are sure it is not hot. If it is hot, use heat-resistant gloves.
3. Always clean glassware thoroughly before putting it away.

Fire Safety

1. Whenever you see this symbol, you will know that you are working with fire. Never use any source of fire without wearing safety goggles.
2. Never heat anything—particularly chemicals—unless instructed to do so.
3. Never heat anything in a closed container.
4. Never reach across a flame.
5. Always use a clamp, tongs, or heat-resistant gloves to handle hot objects.
6. Always maintain a clean work area, particularly when using a flame.

Heat Safety

Whenever you see this symbol, you will know that you should put on heat-resistant gloves to avoid burning your hands.

Chemical Safety

1. Whenever you see this symbol, you will know that you are working with chemicals that could be hazardous.
2. Never smell any chemical directly from its container. Always use your hand to waft some of the odors from the top of the container toward your nose—and only when instructed to do so.
3. Never mix chemicals unless instructed to do so.
4. Never touch or taste any chemical unless instructed to do so.
5. Keep all lids closed when chemicals are not in use. Dispose of all chemicals as instructed by your teacher.

6. Immediately rinse with water any chemicals, particularly acids, that get on your skin and clothes. Then notify your teacher.

Eye and Face Safety

1. Whenever you see this symbol, you will know that you are performing an experiment in which you must take precautions to protect your eyes and face by wearing safety goggles.
2. When you are heating a test tube or bottle, always point it away from you and others. Chemicals can splash or boil out of a heated test tube.

Sharp Instrument Safety

1. Whenever you see this symbol, you will know that you are working with a sharp instrument.
2. Always use single-edged razors; double-edged razors are too dangerous.
3. Handle any sharp instrument with extreme care. Never cut any material toward you; always cut away from you.
4. Immediately notify your teacher if your skin is cut.

Electrical Safety

1. Whenever you see this symbol, you will know that you are using electricity in the laboratory.
2. Never use long extension cords to plug in any electrical device. Do not plug too many appliances into one socket or you may overload the socket and cause a fire.
3. Never touch an electrical appliance or outlet with wet hands.

Animal Safety

1. Whenever you see this symbol, you will know that you are working with live animals.
2. Do not cause pain, discomfort, or injury to an animal.
3. Follow your teacher's directions when handling animals. Wash your hands thoroughly after handling animals or their cages.

One of the first things a scientist learns is that working in the laboratory can be an exciting experience. But the laboratory can also be quite dangerous if proper safety rules are not followed at all times. To prepare yourself for a safe year in the laboratory, read over the following safety rules. Then read them a second time. Make sure you understand each rule. If you do not, ask your teacher to explain any rules you are unsure of.

Dress Code

1. Many materials in the laboratory can cause eye injury. To protect yourself from possible injury, wear safety goggles whenever you are working with chemicals, burners, or any substance that might get into your eyes. Never wear contact lenses in the laboratory.

2. Wear a laboratory apron or coat whenever you are working with chemicals or heated substances.

3. Tie back long hair to keep it away from any chemicals, burners and candles, or other laboratory equipment.

4. Remove or tie back any article of clothing or jewelry that can hang down and touch chemicals and flames.

General Safety Rules

5. Read all directions for an experiment several times. Follow the directions exactly as they are written. If you are in doubt about any part of the experiment, ask your teacher for assistance.

6. Never perform activities that are not authorized by your teacher. Obtain permission before "experimenting" on your own.

7. Never handle any equipment unless you have specific permission.

8. Take extreme care not to spill any material in the laboratory. If a spill occurs, immediately ask your teacher about the proper cleanup procedure. Never simply pour chemicals or other substances into the sink or trash container.

9. Never eat in the laboratory.

10. Wash your hands before and after each experiment.

First Aid

11. Immediately report all accidents, no matter how minor, to your teacher.

12. Learn what to do in case of specific accidents, such as getting acid in your eyes or on your skin. (Rinse acids from your body with lots of water.)

13. Become aware of the location of the first-aid kit. But your teacher should administer any required first aid due to injury. Or your teacher may send you to the school nurse or call a physician.

14. Know where and how to report an accident or fire. Find out the location of the fire extinguisher, phone, and fire alarm. Keep a list of important phone numbers—such as the fire department and the school nurse—near the phone. Immediately report any fires to your teacher.

Heating and Fire Safety

15. Again, never use a heat source, such as a candle or burner, without wearing safety goggles.

16. Never heat a chemical you are not instructed to heat. A chemical that is harmless when cool may be dangerous when heated.

17. Maintain a clean work area and keep all materials away from flames.

18. Never reach across a flame.

19. Make sure you know how to light a Bunsen burner. (Your teacher will demonstrate the proper procedure for lighting a burner.) If the flame leaps out of a burner toward you, immediately turn off the gas. Do not touch the burner. It may be hot. And never leave a lighted burner unattended!

20. When heating a test tube or bottle, always point it away from you and others. Chemicals can splash or boil out of a heated test tube.

21. Never heat a liquid in a closed container. The expanding gases produced may blow the container apart, injuring you or others.

22. Before picking up a container that has been heated, first hold the back of your hand near it. If you can feel the heat on the back of your hand, the container may be too hot to handle. Use a clamp or tongs when handling hot containers.

Using Chemicals Safely

23. Never mix chemicals for the "fun of it." You might produce a dangerous, possibly explosive substance.

24. Never touch, taste, or smell a chemical unless you are instructed by your teacher to do so. Many chemicals are poisonous. If you are instructed to note the fumes in an experiment, gently wave your hand over the opening of a container and direct the fumes toward your nose. Do not inhale the fumes directly from the container.

25. Use only those chemicals needed in the activity. Keep all lids closed when a chemical is not being used. Notify your teacher whenever chemicals are spilled.

26. Dispose of all chemicals as instructed by your teacher. To avoid contamination, never return chemicals to their original containers.

27. Be extra careful when working with acids or bases. Pour such chemicals over the sink, not over your workbench.

28. When diluting an acid, pour the acid into water. Never pour water into an acid.

29. Immediately rinse with water any acids that get on your skin or clothing. Then notify your teacher of any acid spill.

Using Glassware Safely

30. Never force glass tubing into a rubber stopper. A turning motion and lubricant will be helpful when inserting glass tubing into rubber stoppers or rubber tubing. Your teacher will demonstrate the proper way to insert glass tubing.

31. Never heat glassware that is not thoroughly dry. Use a wire screen to protect glassware from any flame.

32. Keep in mind that hot glassware will not appear hot. Never pick up glassware without first checking to see if it is hot. See #22.

33. If you are instructed to cut glass tubing, fire-polish the ends immediately to remove sharp edges.

34. Never use broken or chipped glassware. If glassware breaks, notify your teacher and dispose of the glassware in the proper trash container.

35. Never eat or drink from laboratory glassware. Thoroughly clean glassware before putting it away.

Using Sharp Instruments

36. Handle scalpels or razor blades with extreme care. Never cut material toward you; cut away from you.

37. Immediately notify your teacher if you cut your skin when working in the laboratory.

Animal Safety

38. No experiments that will cause pain, discomfort, or harm to mammals, birds, reptiles, fishes, and amphibians should be done in the classroom or at home.

39. Animals should be handled only if necessary. If an animal is excited or frightened, pregnant, feeding, or with its young, special handling is required.

40. Your teacher will instruct you as to how to handle each animal species that may be brought into the classroom.

41. Clean your hands thoroughly after handling animals or the cage containing animals.

End-of-Experiment Rules

42. After an experiment has been completed, clean up your work area and return all equipment to its proper place.

43. Wash your hands after every experiment.

44. Turn off all burners before leaving the laboratory. Check that the gas line leading to the burner is off as well.

The microscope is an essential tool in the study of life science. It enables you to see things that are too small to be seen with the unaided eye. It also allows you to look more closely at the fine details of larger things.

The microscope you will use in your science class is probably similar to the one illustrated on the following page. This is a compound microscope. It is called compound because it has more than one lens. A simple microscope would contain only one lens. The lenses of the compound microscope are the parts that magnify the object being viewed.

Typically, a compound microscope has one lens in the eyepiece, the part you look through. The eyepiece lens usually has a magnification power of 10X. That is, if you were to look through the eyepiece alone, the object you were viewing would appear 10 times larger than it is.

The compound microscope may contain one or two other lenses. These two lenses are called the low- and high-power objective lenses. The low-power objective lens usually has a magnification of 10X. The high-power objective lens usually has a magnification of 40X. To figure out what the total magnification of your microscope is when using the eyepiece and an objective lens, multiply the powers of the lenses you are using. For example, eyepiece magnification (10X) multiplied by low-power objective lens magnification (10X) = 100X total magnification. What is the total magnification of your microscope using the eyepiece and the high-power objective lens?

To use the microscope properly, it is important to learn the name of each part, its function, and its location on your microscope. Keep the following procedures in mind when using the microscope:

1. Always carry the microscope with both hands. One hand should grasp the arm, and the other should support the base.

2. Place the microscope on the table with the arm toward you. The stage should be facing a light source.

3. Raise the body tube by turning the coarse adjustment knob.

4. Revolve the nosepiece so that the low-power objective lens (10X) is directly in line with the body tube. Click it into place. The low-power lens should be directly over the opening in the stage.

5. While looking through the eyepiece, adjust the diaphragm and the mirror so that the greatest amount of light is coming through the opening in the stage.

6. Place the slide to be viewed on the stage. Center the specimen to be viewed over the hole in the stage. Use the stage clips to hold the slide in position.

7. Look at the microscope from the side rather than through the eyepiece. In this way, you can watch as you use the coarse adjustment knob to lower the body tube until the low-power objective almost touches the slide. Do this slowly so you do not break the slide or damage the lens.

8. Now, looking through the eyepiece, observe the specimen. Use the coarse adjustment knob to raise the body tube, thus raising the low-power objective away from the slide. Continue to raise the body tube until the specimen comes into focus.

9. When viewing a specimen, be sure to keep both eyes open. Though this may seem strange at first, it is really much easier on your eyes. Keeping one eye closed may create a strain, and you might get a headache. Also, if you keep both eyes open, it is easier to draw diagrams of what you are observing. In this way, you do not have to turn your head away from the microscope as you draw.

10. To switch to the high-power objective lens (40X), look at the microscope from the side. Now, revolve the nosepiece so that the high-power objective lens clicks into place. Make sure the lens does not hit the slide.

11. Looking through the eyepiece, use only the fine adjustment knob to bring the specimen into focus. Why should you not use the coarse adjustment knob with the high-power objective?

12. Clean the microscope stage and lens when you are finished. To clean the lenses, use lens paper only. Other types of paper may scratch the lenses.

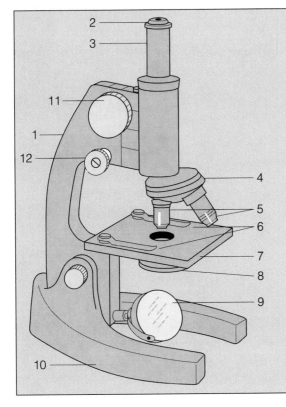

Microscope Parts and Their Functions

1. **Arm** Supports the body tube
2. **Eyepiece** Contains the magnifying lens you look through
3. **Body tube** Maintains the proper distance between the eyepiece and the objective lenses
4. **Nosepiece** Holds the high- and the low-power objective lenses and can be rotated to change magnification
5. **Objective lenses** A low-power lens, which usually provides 10X magnification, and a high-power lens, which usually provides 40X magnification
6. **Stage clips** Hold the slide in place
7. **Stage** Supports the slide being viewed
8. **Diaphragm** Regulates the amount of light let into the body tube
9. **Mirror** Reflects the light upward through the diaphragm, the specimen, and the lenses
10. **Base** Supports the microscope
11. **Coarse adjustment knob** Moves the body tube up and down for focusing
12. **Fine adjustment knob** Moves the body tube slightly to sharpen the image

The laboratory balance is an important tool in scientific investigations. You can use the balance to determine the mass of materials that you study or experiment with in the laboratory.

Different kinds of balances are used in the laboratory. One kind of balance is the double-pan balance. Another kind of balance is the Triple-beam balance. The balance that you may use in your science class is probably similar to one of the balances illustrated in this Appendix. To use the balance properly, you should learn the name, function, and location of each part of the balance you are using. What kind of balance do you have in your science class?

The Double-Pan Balance

The double-pan balance shown in this Appendix has two beams. Some double-pan balances have only one beam. The beams are calibrated, or marked, in grams. The upper beam is divided into ten major units of 1 gram each. Each of these units is further divided into units of 1/10 of a gram. The lower beam is divided into twenty units, and each unit is equal to 10 grams. The lower beam can be used to find the masses of objects up to 200 grams. Each beam has a rider that is moved to the right along the beam. The rider indicates the number of grams needed to balance the object in the left pan. What is the total mass the balance can measure?

Before using the balance, you should be sure that the pans are empty and both riders are pointing to zero. The balance should be on a flat, level surface. The pointer should be at the zero point. If your pointer does not read zero, slowly turn the adjustment knob so that the pointer does read zero.

The following procedure can be used to find the mass of an object with a double-pan balance:

1. Place the object whose mass is to be determined on the left pan.

2. Move the rider on the lower beam to the 10-gram notch.

3. If the pointer moves to the right of the zero point on the scale, the object has a mass less than

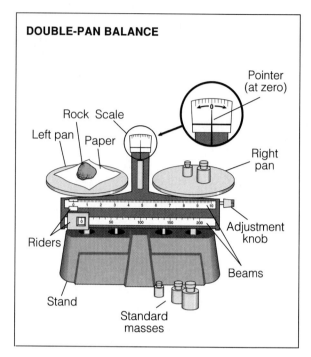

DOUBLE-PAN BALANCE

Parts of a Double-Pan Balance and Their Functions

Pointer   Indicator used to determine when the mass being measured is balanced by the riders or masses of the balance

Scale   Series of marks along which the pointer moves

Zero Point   Center line of the scale to which the pointer moves when the mass being measured is balanced by the riders or masses of the balance

Adjustment Knob   Knob used to set the balance at the zero point when the riders are all on zero and no masses are on either pan

Left Pan   Platform on which an object whose mass is to be determined is placed

Right Pan   Platform on which standard masses are placed

Beams   Horizontal strips of metal on which marks, or graduations, appear that indicate grams or parts of grams

Riders   Devices that are moved along the beams and used to balance the object being measured and to determine its mass

Stand   Support for the balance

10 grams. Return the rider on the lower beam to zero. Slowly move the rider on the upper beam until the pointer is at zero. The reading on the beam is the mass of the object.

4. If the pointer did not move to the right of the zero, move the rider on the lower beam notch by notch until the pointer does move to the right. Move the rider back one notch. Then move the rider on the upper beam until the pointer is at zero. The sum of the readings on both beams is the mass of the object.

5. If the two riders are moved completely to the right side of the beams and the pointer remains to the left of the zero point, the object has a mass greater than the total mass that the balance can measure.

The total mass that most double-pan balances can measure is 210 grams. If an object has a mass greater than 210 grams, return the riders to the zero point.

The following procedure can be used to find the mass of an object greater than 210 grams:

1. Place the standard masses on the right pan one at a time, starting with the largest, until the pointer remains to the right of the zero point.

2. Remove one of the large standard masses and replace it with a smaller one. Continue replacing the standard masses with smaller ones until the pointer remains to the left of the zero point. When the pointer remains to the left of the zero point, the mass of the object on the left pan is greater than the total mass of the standard masses on the right pan.

3. Move the rider on the lower beam and then the rider on the upper beam until the pointer stops at the zero point on the scale. The mass of the object is equal to the sum of the readings on the beams plus the mass of the standard masses. ance at the zero point when the riders are all on zero and no masses are on either pan

The Triple-Beam Balance

The Triple-beam balance is a single-pan balance with three beams calibrated in grams. The front, or 100-gram, beam is divided into ten units of 10 grams each. The middle, or 500-gram, beam is divided into five units of 100 grams each. The back, or 10-gram is divided into ten major units of 1 gram each. Each of these units is further divided into units of 1/10 of a gram. What is the largest mass you could find with a triple-beam balance?

The following procedure can be used to find the mass of an object with a triple-beam balance:

1. Place the object on the pan.

2. Move the rider on the middle beam notch by notch until the horizontal pointer drops below zero. Move the rider back one notch.

3. Move the rider on the front beam notch by notch until the pointer again drops below zero. Move the rider back one notch.

4. Slowly slide the rider along the back beam until the pointer stops at the zero point.

5. The mass of the object is equal to the sum of the readings on the three beams.

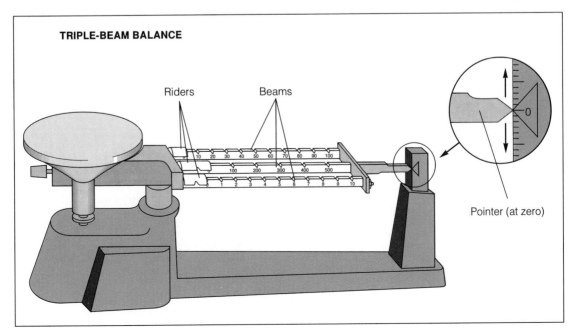

TRIPLE-BEAM BALANCE

Riders   Beams

Pointer (at zero)

Appendix F

THE CHEMICAL ELEMENTS

NAME	SYMBOL	ATOMIC NUMBER	ATOMIC MASS†
Actinium	Ac	89	(227)
Aluminum	Al	13	27.0
Americium	Am	95	(243)
Antimony	Sb	51	121.8
Argon	Ar	18	39.9
Arsenic	As	33	74.9
Astatine	At	85	(210)
Barium	Ba	56	137.3
Berkelium	Bk	97	(247)
Beryllium	Be	4	9.01
Bismuth	Bi	83	209.0
Boron	B	5	10.8
Bromine	Br	35	79.9
Cadmium	Cd	48	112.4
Calcium	Ca	20	40.1
Californium	Cf	98	(251)
Carbon	C	6	12.01
Cerium	Ce	58	140.1
Cesium	Cs	55	132.9
Chlorine	Cl	17	35.5
Chromium	Cr	24	52.0
Cobalt	Co	27	58.9
Copper	Cu	29	63.5
Curium	Cm	96	(247)
Dysprosium	Dy	66	162.5
Einsteinium	Es	99	(254)
Erbium	Er	68	167.3
Europium	Eu	63	152.0
Fermium	Fm	100	(257)
Fluorine	F	9	19.0
Francium	Fr	87	(223)
Gadolinium	Gd	64	157.2
Gallium	Ga	31	69.7
Germanium	Ge	32	72.6
Gold	Au	79	197.0
Hafnium	Hf	72	178.5
Helium	He	2	4.00
Holmium	Ho	67	164.9
Hydrogen	H	1	1.008
Indium	In	49	114.8
Iodine	I	53	126.9
Iridium	Ir	77	192.2
Iron	Fe	26	55.8
Krypton	Kr	36	83.8
Lanthanum	La	57	138.9
Lawrencium	Lr	103	(256)
Lead	Pb	82	207.2
Lithium	Li	3	6.94
Lutetium	Lu	71	175.0
Magnesium	Mg	12	24.3
Manganese	Mn	25	54.9
Mendelevium	Md	101	(258)
Mercury	Hg	80	200.6
Molybdenum	Mo	42	95.9
Neodymium	Nd	60	144.2
Neon	Ne	10	20.2
Neptunium	Np	93	(237)
Nickel	Ni	28	58.7
Niobium	Nb	41	92.9
Nitrogen	N	7	14.01
Nobelium	No	102	(255)
Osmium	Os	76	190.2
Oxygen	O	8	16.00
Palladium	Pd	46	106.4
Phosphorus	P	15	31.0
Platinum	Pt	78	195.1
Plutonium	Pu	94	(244)
Polonium	Po	84	(210)
Potassium	K	19	39.1
Praseodymium	Pr	59	140.9
Promethium	Pm	61	(145)
Protactinium	Pa	91	(231)
Radium	Ra	88	(226)
Radon	Rn	86	(222)
Rhenium	Re	75	186.2
Rhodium	Rh	45	102.9
Rubidium	Rb	37	85.5
Ruthenium	Ru	44	101.1
Samarium	Sm	62	150.4
Scandium	Sc	21	45.0
Selenium	Se	34	79.0
Silicon	Si	14	28.1
Silver	Ag	47	107.9
Sodium	Na	11	23.0
Strontium	Sr	38	87.6
Sulfur	S	16	32.1
Tantalum	Ta	73	180.9
Technetium	Tc	43	(97)
Tellurium	Te	52	127.6
Terbium	Tb	65	158.9
Thallium	Tl	81	204.4
Thorium	Th	90	232.0
Thulium	Tm	69	168.9
Tin	Sn	50	118.7
Titanium	Ti	22	47.9
Tungsten	W	74	183.9
Unnilennium	Une	109	(266?)
Unnilhexium	Unh	106	(263)
Unniloctium	Uno	108	(265)
Unnilpentium	Unp	105	(262)
Unnilquadium	Unq	104	(261)
Unnilseptium	Uns	107	(262)
Uranium	U	92	238.0
Vanadium	V	23	50.9
Xenon	Xe	54	131.3
Ytterbium	Yb	70	173.0
Yttrium	Y	39	88.9
Zinc	Zn	30	65.4
Zirconium	Zr	40	91.2

†Numbers in parentheses give the mass number of the most stable isotope.

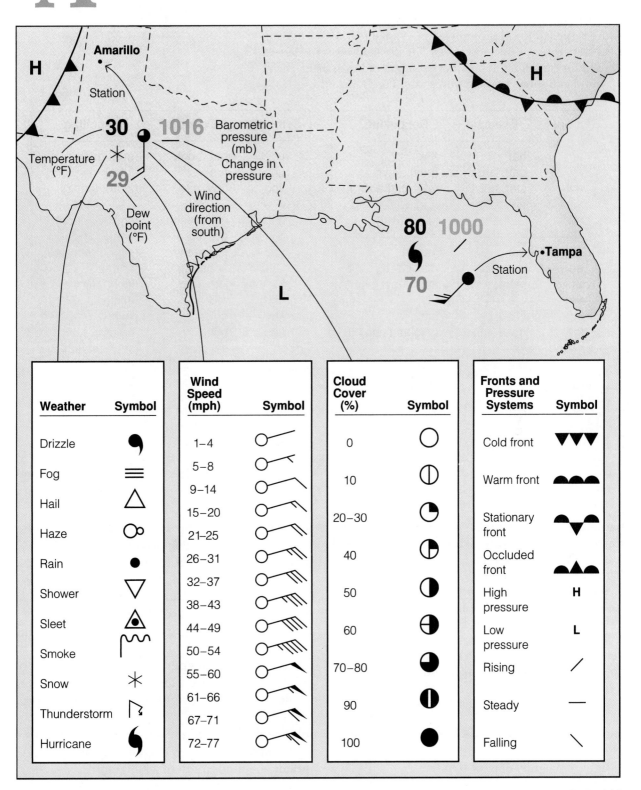

Amarillo

Station

30

1016 — Barometric pressure (mb)

Change in pressure

Temperature (°F)

29

Dew point (°F)

Wind direction (from south)

H

L

80 1000

70

•Tampa

Station

H

Weather	Symbol
Drizzle	
Fog	
Hail	
Haze	
Rain	
Shower	
Sleet	
Smoke	
Snow	
Thunderstorm	
Hurricane	

Wind Speed (mph)	Symbol
1–4	
5–8	
9–14	
15–20	
21–25	
26–31	
32–37	
38–43	
44–49	
50–54	
55–60	
61–66	
67–71	
72–77	

Cloud Cover (%)	Symbol
0	
10	
20–30	
40	
50	
60	
70–80	
90	
100	

Fronts and Pressure Systems	Symbol
Cold front	
Warm front	
Stationary front	
Occluded front	
High pressure	H
Low pressure	L
Rising	/
Steady	—
Falling	\

Glossary

Pronunciation Key

When difficult names or terms first appear in the text, they are respelled to aid pronunciation. A syllable in SMALL CAPITAL LETTERS receives the most stress. The key below lists the letters used for respelling. It includes examples of words using each sound and shows how the words would be respelled.

Symbol	Example	Respelling
a	hat	(hat)
ay	pay, late	(pay), (layt)
ah	star, hot	(stahr), (haht)
ai	air, dare	(air), (dair)
aw	law, all	(law), (awl)
eh	met	(meht)
ee	bee, eat	(bee), (eet)
er	learn, sir, fur	(lern), (ser), (fer)
ih	fit	(fiht)
igh	mile, sigh	(mighl), (sigh)
oh	no	(noh)
oi	soil, boy	(soil), (boi)
oo	root, rule	(root), (rool)
or	born, door	(born), (dor)
ow	plow, out	(plow), (owt)

Symbol	Example	Respelling
u	put, book	(put), (buk)
uh	fun	(fuhn)
yoo	few, use	(fyoo), (yooz)
ch	chill, reach	(chihl), (reech)
g	go, dig	(goh), (dihg)
j	jet, gently, bridge	(jeht), (JEHNT-lee), (brihj)
k	kite, cup	(kight), (kuhp)
ks	mix	(mihks)
kw	quick	(kwihk)
ng	bring	(brihng)
s	say, cent	(say), (sehnt)
sh	she, crash	(shee), (krash)
th	three	(three)
y	yet, onion	(yeht), (UHN-yuhn)
z	zip, always	(zihp), (AWL-wayz)
zh	treasure	(TREH-zher)

barometer: instrument that measures air pressure

bathyscaph (BATH-ih-skaf): self-propelled submarine observatory

bathysphere (BATH-ih-sfeer): small, sphere-shaped diving vessel used for underwater research

Celsius: temperature scale in which there are 100 degrees between the freezing and boiling points of water

centimeter: one-hundredth of a meter

control: an experiment run without a variable in order to show that any data from the experimental setup was due to the variable being tested

compound light microscope: microscope having more than one lens and that uses a beam of light to magnify objects

conversion factor: fraction that always equals one, which is used for dimensional analysis

cubic centimeter: metric unit used to measure the volume of solids; equal to a milliliter

data: recorded observations and measurements

density: mass per unit volume of a substance

dimensional analysis: method of converting one unit to another

electromagnetic spectrum: arrangement of electromagnetic waves that includes visible light, ultraviolet light, infrared light, X-rays, and radio waves

electron microscope: microscope that uses a beam of electrons to magnify an object

gram: one-thousandth of a kilogram

hypothesis (high-PAHTH-uh-sihs): a proposed solution to a scientific problem

infrared telescope: telescope that gathers infrared light from distant objects in order to produce an image of that object

kilogram: basic unit of mass in the metric system

kilometer: one thousand meters

law: a basic scientific theory that has been tested many times and is generally accepted as true by the scientific community

lens: any transparent material that bends light passing through it

light-year: distance light travels in a year

liter: basic unit of volume in the metric system

meter: basic unit of length in the metric system

metric system: standard system of measurement used by all scientists

milligram: one-thousandth of a gram

milliliter: one-thousandth of a liter

millimeter: one-thousandth of a meter

newton: basic unit of weight in the metric system

radio telescope: telescope that gathers radio waves from distant objects in order to produce an image of that object

reflecting telescope: telescope that uses a series of mirrors to gather and focus visible light from distant objects

refracting telescope: telescope that uses a series of lenses to gather and focus visible light from distant objects

scientific method: a systematic approach to problem solving

seismograph (SIGHZ-muh-grahf): instrument that detects and measures earthquake waves

theory: a logical, time-tested explanation for events that occur in the natural world

ultraviolet telescope: telescope that gathers ultraviolet light from distant objects in order to produce an image of the object

variable: the factor being tested in an experimental setup

weight: measure of the gravitational attraction between objects

X-ray telescope: telescope that gathers X-rays from distant objects in order to produce an image of that object

Index